D1611981

Triple Crown Plus

IVAN MAUGER
with
PETER OAKES

PELHAM BOOKS

First published in Great Britain by
PELHAM BOOKS LTD
52 Bedford Square
London, W.C.1
AUGUST 1971
SECOND IMPRESSION JANUARY 1972

7207 0528 2

Printed lithographically in Great Britain by Hollen Street Press Ltd at Slough and bound by James Burn at Esher, Surrey

Contents

Illustrations

ACKNOWLEDGEMENTS

The author's thanks are due to the following whose photographs are reproduced in this book:

Evening Citizen, Glasgow: 6.
Franz Kellworth, Munich: 8.
Wright Wood: 10, 12, 15, 16, 19.
A. C. Weedon: 11, 13, 14, 17.
R. S. Oliver: 18.
J. E. Harvey: 20.
C. & R. J. Lawrence: 23.

I

Triumph . . . Friday, September 6th, 1968

It was a mild September evening. The crisp Swedish air made it pleasant to sit out in the open.

Back in England heavy rain had waterlogged the Pennycross track and forced the Plymouth promoters to postpone their prestige Bromley Bowl individual event.

There were no such climatic problems in Sweden. The strikingly baroque Ullevi Stadium was waiting to crown a new World Champion.

Swedish folk hero Ove Fundin – with five World titles behind him – knew that the title he had so valiantly won in 1967 was slipping away from him.

He had scored only four points from his first four rides, and was faced with a final four laps of the red shale circuit knowing that no matter where he finished, his world crown had slipped away.

Within five minutes a new World Champion would be crowned.

And I knew that within five minutes that new World Champion could be . . . me!

The afternoon sun was setting in the evening sky as I coasted up to the tapes for what was my last race in the 1968 World Championship Final.

It was Heat 19. World Final. Friday, 6th September. I knew as I rolled round the track – glancing up to the stand where my wife was sitting – that I needed at least a second place to make the eleven years of suffering worth while.

A second place – and the two points it would bring – would put me out of touch with my closest rival. Two points and I could call myself World Speedway Champion.

Nervously I edged towards the tapes. England number one Nigel Boocock was in the race. So too was hard-riding Swedish hope Torbjorn Harryson. And Polish star Jerzy Trzeszkowski.

Four times this evening I have made the gate. Everything co-ordinated I have been first into the first bend. I have been able to choose my line. Make my own race. And four times I have been first past the chequered flag. The cannon that signals the finish of four laps has resounded happily in my ears.

But all that can mean nothing unless I pick up my two points. It is impossible to explain – or to try to explain – what I felt as the weights on either side of the starting gate clumped into position.

Underneath me my trusty steed ticked merrily away. Guy Allott, my engine tuner, had done a good job. I knew that.

My two mechanics, Bob Hall and Tony Shelley, had changed the rear tyre.

Everything, I knew, depended on me. The tapes flew up and precisely 78 seconds later the cannon sounded for the fifth time in my ears.

It would be easy to say that actually winning the World Championship was something of an anti-climax after the build-up that had really been constructed on foundations laid more than 15 years earlier.

But it wasn't an anti-climax. Maybe it took some time really to sink in that I had reached the very top of my profession. But anti-climax it was not.

It is a feeling I can share only with my wife and those riders who have experienced it before. As I went to mount the rostrum to receive the silver winged wheel, the trophy, and the laurels, I was in a daze.

And it wasn't until some days later that I really appreciated what had happened.

It was then that I began to realise what a long, and winding road it had been to that success at Ullevi.

A road that had begun in a quiet suburb of Christchurch, New Zealand, when I was just a schoolboy.

2

At the Grass Roots

It all really began when, as a youngster, I was keen on cycle speedway.

First of all, I think I should make it quite clear that riding my cycle speedway bike never helped me one ounce in riding my speedway bike in later years.

There is absolutely no comparison between the two because in cycle speedway you are riding with no power around the corners and in speedway it is all power around the corners.

The fact that so many riders seem to progress from cycle speedway to full-time speedway is just one of those facts of sporting life. It is, I suppose, the equivalent of the countless soccer stars who will talk of makeshift games played on waste-land or bombed sites.

To say they made the grade in top class soccer because they played such impromptu games would be foolish. Just as it would be foolish to try and pretend that speedway stars are born on the makeshift cycle speedway tracks of the world.

I do, however, believe that cycle speedway – and in particular the way I rode cycle speedway – was to be a great benefit to me in future years.

When I was about ten or maybe eleven I suppose I was riding cycle speedway and at that time it was booming in my hometown of Christchurch in New Zealand's South Island.

Every suburb had two or three tracks running and there was intense rivalry among the schoolchildren of the districts. Leagues were in operation in Christchurch and everything was finely organised in districts and suburbs.

I was in what was known as the 'C' grade in my local suburb and I was only a reserve but I was very keen on cycle speedway.

My mates and I were all enthusiastic and to get on we built a track for ourselves. Of course it was a bit of an adventure for us to build our own track but even so we had to work a great deal on it.

I was only a schoolkid at the time, getting a couple of shillings a week in pocket-money, so it was a matter of having to build up my own bike.

Everyone was in the same position and I can remember the great pride I took in building up a bike of my own. When I somehow obtained an old rusty wheel I would really spend hours and hours cleaning it up. It was pretty hard really as we were only kids and the pocket money certainly didn't stretch to new bikes – or even new wheels!

We were all very, very keen but I would go as far as to say I was keener than any of the others – in our suburb anyway. For three or four years during the school holidays I can remember going out on to the local cycle speedway track and either riding round and round for hours on end or working in the pits and making bits of safety fence with wooden boxes and things like that.

Sometimes the other kids would help me but mostly I would do it on my own. I really sacrificed a lot. I never went to the beaches in the summer or things like that – I was only interested in cycle speedway every day.

Later on, when I started riding on ordinary speedway, naturally I only had enough money to buy an old heap (as everyone did in those days to get going). The fact that it was, and I had to pull it to bits to try and make something out of it, never bothered me at all.

Even if I spent days and days doing it, I didn't mind because I had been used to doing this sort of thing during my cycle speedway days. I really went to great pains in those days to get my cycle speedway bike going and that was one of the big things that helped me when I eventually came to speedway.

When I first came to England with my wife Raye, we didn't have very much money as I was only riding once a week – and occasionally not even once a week. Sometimes I didn't get a ride, so did not have enough money to buy new parts for my bike.

I think in normal circumstances I would have given speedway up a hundred times in England and gone back to New Zealand and started working again, but I was so keen on riding and accustomed to working for a long time in order to get on a track for a minute or so that it didn't really bother me.

Even in those cycle speedway days I wanted to succeed and those many hours spent on the track without even a friend to encourage me, made a considerable difference to my outlook.

I realised – even as a schoolboy – that no one will succeed at anything unless he is willing to devote a lot of time to it.

It was while I was at school in Christchurch that I began to make steady progress in the cycle speedway world.

I rode for my local suburb Woolston and was eventually selected to ride by my town, the State and by the South Island national side.

Cycle speedway was my major interest at school and I am not giving away any school-age secrets when I say that I was far more proficient outside a classroom than inside.

Besides my antics on the home-made cycle speedway tracks I was also quite keen on running and won the provincial championship at the 220 yard sprint at school grade.

I became Christchurch All-Schoolboy Sprint Champion and was at one time seriously considering trying to make myself a career in athletics. But running was always to remain one of my lesser loves.

While at school I also played tennis, hockey and rugby union and was fortunate enough to be picked for both my province (Canterbury) and South Island at both rugger and hockey.

I was lucky in some respects that both my parents were keen on sport in general and speedway in particular.

My ancestors had settled in New Zealand after sailing cross the oceans from the family home on the Channel Islands during the middle of the 19th century.

The name Mauger (pronounced Major) is a direct derivation of the Norwegian Magor and was later changed to Maghor and eventually Mauger by ancestors in the Channel Islands.

Even to this day there are families with the name Mauger in the Channel Isles – the only place other than New Zealand where I have ever heard the name.

My ancestors quickly settled in Christchurch and made the cathedral town their homeplace. My father, Edwin Arthur Mauger, and his wife Alice Rita became firm speedway fans when it started up just after the second world war and to some extent my elder brother Trevor, my sister Pat and myself became accustomed to the roar of dirt bikes from the time we were old enough to be wheeled along to the local track in a pram.

Trev in fact has done quite a lot of riding himself and I'm convinced that but for a serious injury he would have been a better rider than I am. Certainly as a youngster he was better!

I transferred from cycle speedway to speedway proper as soon as I was old enough to have a licence to race which, in New Zealand, is 15.

At school I had also been pretty keen on roller-skating and in New Zealand a popular game was roller-hockey – hockey on roller skates. It was quite a highly organised sport in Christchurch and I belonged to a local team that competed in a league set-up.

One of my team-mates' father was a speedway rider of some talent and a local performer at the Christchurch track. It was through the friendship with his son that I got to know Windy Rees and eventually I bought his old Jap and decided to give it a go myself.

At first I was worried about what Mum and Dad would think but eventually I plucked up the courage and told them that I wanted to be a speedway rider.

Admittedly it wasn't quite as easy as that. But Mum and Dad didn't put up too much opposition and they quickly became my keenest fans.

I had my first ever meeting on a Saturday in one of the novice events at the quarter-mile Aranui track in Christchurch, on, I think, 2nd October, 1956.

I was still very keen on athletics and would often spend a Saturday afternoon running on a local track and then slip out of my vest and shorts into speedway leathers so that I could take part in the Saturday evening meeting at Aranui!

As I expected, I eventually had to decide to concentrate on one sport and it was a question – athletics or speedway? Speedway won although I am still not really certain why I chose the mechanical sport as opposed to the strictly physical sport.

Certainly athletics would have been cheaper and I had certainly achieved far more success on the quarter-mile running track than the quarter mile speedway track!

Rides were few and far between in New Zealand and I spent the entire 1956 season competing in novice events on the same programme as big name heroes like Geoff Mardon, Barry Briggs and Ronnie Moore.

I was still very much a raw, green inexperienced novice and I dare say some of my friends thought I was a little bit big-headed when I announced that I was ready to sail to England to take the British speedway scene by storm.

I'd seen Ronnie Moore come home with all the trappings of success – the big car, the fancy clothes, the expensive bikes – and I thought it would all be so easy.

Raye and I had known each other since we had been introduced by a friend at school and we quickly became very attached to each other. After talking it all over Raye agreed that I should go to England and we asked our parents if we could get married before we were due to sail out of Christchurch.

Happily we both had understanding parents who didn't stand in our way and we were married in 1956.

Instead of the usual honeymoon we saved all our money to pay the fare to come to England and by the time we had collected enough to meet the cost of the boat trip it was 1957 and we were expecting our first child.

In fact Raye was pregnant while we made the boat trip and Julie was born in Fulham Hospital on July 10th, 1957, and instead of two mouths to feed we had three.

It was with the knowledge that we would soon become parents that we left New Zealand for England. I suppose, looking back, it was the fact that we were still young and a trip to England represented an adventure that persuaded us to risk it.

To some extent Raye was coming back home and it may have been that which helped us make up our mind to risk our marriage and our life's savings on a trip across.

Raye had been born in Carlisle, and had emigrated to New Zealand with her family when she was eight so she could still remember something about England and it wasn't quite the same as sailing across the world to a completely strange land.

Raye also had some relatives still living in England so at least we knew that we could find friends somewhere.

But as far as speedway was concerned I was venturing very much out of my depth and I later realised that there is a great deal of difference between riding in a couple of novice events at a track in New Zealand and riding for a team in what was the strongest league in the world of speedway.

We were both willing to risk it though, so we packed the few belongings we had accumulated in a year's marriage and set off on the big adventure . . . to England.

3

A Fanfare of Trumpets . . . and Despair

I arrived in Britain a few days before Easter, 1957.

Ready to make my fame and fortune on the English speedway tracks. And it all looked so easy.

I was given a fanfare of trumpets, figuratively if not literally, as I was heralded as a future World Champion.

Everywhere I went I was treated regally. The new sensation. The seventeen-year-old who was going to conquer the world within weeks.

While I still feel that the initial publicity my arrival in England attracted didn't give me premature hopes of greatness, I certainly believe it led the fans into believing I was something that I was not.

Wimbledon promoter Ronnie Greene certainly proved that when it comes to publicity he has few equals and no superiors. The local Wimbledon papers, the Speedway magazines and the national press descended on me as if I was to be the new Messiah.

I suppose they thought back to a few years previous when another young Christchurch product sailed into England. He, too, was 17 when he first arrived at Plough Lane.

Within a few months that fresh-faced lad had crowned his first season in Britain by becoming the youngest-ever World Finalist. His name . . . Ronnie Moore.

And everything I read in those first few days in London was the same – Wimbledon's new Ronnie Moore arrives.

If this publicity had built up my hopes and threatened to elevate me to a plane on which I had no right to be, I was quickly brought back down to earth when I took part in my first practice lap of the Wimbledon track.

It was practice day on Saturday, 13th April, 1957 and the weather held out. A thousand or so fans had sneaked into the stadium to have their first taste of a new season's sport. The fact that it was nothing more than a limbering up exercise did little to hide their glee at seeing the bikes in action again.

As the new wonder boy I was very much at the centre of the limelight even though World class riders like Barry Briggs, Ron How and Cyril Maidment were at the practice.

I felt as if all eyes were on me as I gingerly went out for my first lap. I found the track easy and good to ride and managed to make a fairly impressive gate in my first outing and by the time I'd completed four laps I felt quite pleased with myself.

A week later I picked up the *Speedway Star & News* and read: 'Ivan Mauger – from the gate he was as good as most riders on parade. His cornering though was slow and another fault that must be remedied if he hopes to make real progress is a tendency to ride the centre of the track all the time.'

I knew after reading this that there was a lot of difference between showing up well in novice events at Aranui and making a name for myself in England!

However that first practice must have impressed the Wimbledon boss Ronnie Greene for he told me I'd be in the Dons side to meet a Polish international team in the opening match of the season the following Friday.

What a start I thought – and the chance to produce that mind-blowing, dream-making debut. That sort of debut, though, belongs to the pages of the *Boys' Own Annual* and certainly I wasn't plucked straight out of bound volumes.

The Polish meeting was something that is hard to forget. Not so much because I scored three points on my debut but because of the furore that surrounded it.

First of all, the Polish boys missed a special practice that had been laid on for them because of problems getting the cross-Channel ferry after a drive across Europe.

When they did arrive it was discovered it wasn't really a test team – instead the Sparta club side. A good side – but not good enough to tax what was rightly considered the strongest side in Britain.

Very quickly it was obvious that the Poles weren't going to provide too stiff opposition.

For a start they only had seven men for what was programmed as an eight-man match. And they only had six machines! By the end of the meeting that number had been halved as the eager but relatively unskilled Polish boys found it easier to hit the fence than to keep going in a straight line.

After about six heats the Wimbledon management decided the match was too one-sided and promptly handicapped all the Wimbledon side by 40 yards. This didn't please the Poles (I don't think it would have pleased any side being made to look like mere novices) and after a monumental row the idea was scrapped and the one race completed under the handicap system scrubbed and re-run.

Anyway, I finished my first official meeting with three points . . . on a winning side . . . with a memory that would last a life-time. I thought I'd done reasonably well considering my lack of experience but I knew that I was a long way off being another Ronnie Moore.

The publicity kept going. I probably had more column inches than any other raw novice in speedway's history and when I found my photograph on the front cover of the national speedway magazine I rushed out to buy half a dozen copies to post them air mail to my folks back in New Zealand.

The publicity built up . . . but the number of rides I had started to drop. I was missing from Wimbledon's side for their opening Britannia Cup meeting and found myself guesting for Oxford in my first ever trip past Birmingham.

I had to drive up to Liverpool where former rider Reg Duval had re-opened the Stanley Stadium for a series of challenge matches against National League sides.

Oxford, a man short, asked if they could use me and even though I only got one point I was quite pleased when experienced speedway journalist Frank McLean wrote: 'Ivan Mauger tried hard, but appears to need just that much more experience on the track before he can make any headway.'

At least I wasn't outclassed and I felt that Frank's verdict was a just one. What I needed was the experience.

Experience. The key-note to it all. And he might have added – the cash to buy a new bike. The machine I had wasn't really in the pink of condition that was needed if I was to compete on level terms with the rest of the Wimbledon team.

But there was nothing I could do about it. While I wasn't penniless I certainly didn't have any spare cash for a new speedway bike.

Besides the few bob I was earning with one, maybe two, rides a week in the second half at Wimbledon I was also getting £7 a week as one of the stadium's groundsmen.

I'd be down at the track at seven in the morning and work throughout the day making sure that everything was spick and span for the Monday night meetings.

Another second half lad, Gil Goldfinch, who later died tragically at his home, was also on the groundstaff and we were both as keen as mustard to succeed in the sport.

Often I would be out on the track with my bike before most people had left for work, riding around and around trying to pick up the knowledge and experience to break into the side.

By June I'd ridden, I think, only once for Wimbledon since the opening meeting and I decided it was time I broadened my horizon and started riding elsewhere.

Looking around it was obvious that the only real source of extra rides and valuable experience was the Southern Area League – for long a breeding ground of new talent and, as it was to prove a couple of years later, the launching pad for most of the Southern-based Provincial League sides.

My first meeting outside the senior league was on Saturday, 8th June at the Tongham Stadium, home of S.A.L. side Aldershot. They were running the individual Whitsun Cup and I was invited to take part along with pal Gil Goldfinch, Ernie Baker, at that time mechanic to Barry Briggs, and another of the boys who had the occasional second half ride at Wimbledon; Ross Gilbertson and Covent Garden porter Pat Flanagan.

Sixteen of us lined up and from a series of qualifying heats the top four scorers went through into the final. I wasn't one of the four and found it hard getting my three points.

A fortnight later I was back at Aldershot, this time for the June Cup, and was able to show some improvement. By now I was getting accustomed to the track and scored six points which put me into one of the two semi-finals.

I was particularly happy about that because I got my six points from three rides – and in the first of those three I fell while leading eventual winner Jimmy Heard who laid it down brilliantly behind me to avoid what might have been my first nasty accident.

I was still riding in the second half at Plough Lane and before the end of the season had another ride for the Wimbledon side and managed to get just one point.

It was obvious to me that I wasn't going to be an overnight sensation but I felt that slowly I was improving and perhaps if I had been given more opportunities I might have settled into something like a decent form.

Rye House was the next track to give me rides and I rode for them in a couple of Southern Area League matches. I made my debut for them at Rayleigh against Rayleigh Rovers – at the time Rayleigh had two sides, one in the National League and the other in the S.A.L. – and even though I scored only four points there was some consolation in the fact that I was near the top of the scorers in a disastrously heavy defeat. A team-mate then was Brian Brett who was be be partnered with me when I came back to England and Newcastle five seasons later! Also beginning at Rye House at that time was a young novice who later became a star of the Provincial League and then the British League . . . Colin Pratt.

I was beginning to get a few more rides by mid-summer although nowhere near as many as I would have liked and to some extent I still felt that I deserved a break in the Wimbledon team. But what chance had I of getting into a side that included Briggo, Ron How, Cyril Maidment, Gerry Jackson, Cyril Brine, Split Waterman and Bob Andrews?

There was certainly a tremendous gap between the Southern Area League and the Wimbledon lower end and I was finding it terribly hard to bridge the gap.

Twice I turned in pretty good performances in open meetings – I got seven points in the Sussex Championship at Eastbourne and then nine points for a London Select side at non-league Bradford – but I was still waiting for a lengthy run in the Dons side.

I began to realise it wouldn't come and when Phil Bishop offered me the chance of a trip to Holland to compete in the famed Golden Helmet series during August I jumped at the chance.

As early as 1957 I had realised that the more experience I could gain racing on the Continent the more chance I had of success and while some riders were reluctant to travel anywhere unknown I was always eager to taste racing outside England.

I scoured the columns of the speedway press every week and whenever I saw a mention of meetings outside Britain I would make a quick phone call to try and find out a bit more.

It was probably this which made it so easy for me to travel from continent to continent in later years. I will always be grateful to Phil Bishop for that Dutch trip and his untimely death in that dreadful Lokeren Mini-bus disaster in 1970 which cost not only

Phil's life but that of riders Pete Bradshaw, Martyn Piddock and Malcolm Carmichael, meant I had lost a very good friend.

I will always remember Phil and how he took me under his wing on that trip as we raced in Hengelo, the magnificent Olympic Stadium in Amsterdam; Tilburg and the Sleen Sports Park. It was a strange twist of fate that cost Phil his life coming back from Tilburg, fourteen years later on a trip that he had made countless times.

As always on this trip he was the showman and it was typical of Phil that I was programmed as a South African international even though I'd never been to the country! It was a happy trip punctuated by many funny episodes.

Between my Dutch excursion and the end of the season in October I only had two more official meetings – both in the Rye House colours in Southern Area League clashes with Aldershot.

At least I *should* say one and a half matches, for I didn't arrive for the first one until the match was half-way over! Huge traffic jams between London and Hertfordshire on Sunday, 8th September meant that team-mate Ronnie Rolfe and I didn't get to the stadium until the meeting was well on its way and we changed in the car on the way to the track. By the time I got there I only had one ride left and picked up a third place. I don't really want to remember too much about that meeting because it was only 24 hours after I had failed to score at Aldershot in the first leg on the home-and-away meeting.

I didn't feel too bad when the season finished at Wimbledon as I felt I was a little better than I had been in Christchurch. Much of the early-season publicity had waned and I was being allowed to carry on in my own sweet way. I had a disappointing end to the year when I rode badly in Wimbledon's Junior Cup – a meeting which I might have been expected to win – but all in all it hadn't been such a bad season.

I'd not made any money out of speedway – in fact once Raye had recovered from the birth of Julie she had to go out to work to pay for our tiny flat in Wimbledon.

I couldn't afford a car and had to run about in an old van and rode a beaten up old bike that I used to paint silver before every meeting so that it would look better than it was!

We did however make lots of friends in that first season – true friends who helped us out during our most difficult years. Ken Vale, the late Peter Arnold, supporters Sid and Rene in particular tried to make us feel at home and often Ken and his wife would come round on a Sunday morning, tell Raye and myself to drop what we were doing and take us out into the country.

This friendship, more than anything else, made the 1957 season worthwhile and I was also able to indulge in a little bit of cycle speedway as captain of the local South London Hunters who rode in Garrett Park, a stone's throw from Wimbledon's Earlsfield Station!

Raye has always been a great help to me throughout my career starting from those very early days when we didn't have a lot of money.

I know from travelling around that a lot of wives are against their husbands riding speedway and to some extent I can understand this because it is a dangerous sport and it can't be easy for a wife to sit up in the stands and watch her husband go out on a track every week risking his life or serious injury.

In Raye's case speedway was her husband's occupation but to me it was a way of life from the time I first went on my local track at Aranui.

It was probably the only life I wanted and Raye had to go through some hardships just for me. I went through these hardships because I wanted to and because I wanted to be a speedway rider.

She had to come over to England and take a drastic drop in living conditions just because *I* wanted to be a speedway rider. But she never complained and went out to work in a supermarket and later a watch factory to earn money so that I could continue riding in Britain.

The money I was earning on speedway and working at Wimbledon stadium during 1957 and later 1958 certainly wasn't enough to keep us going, particularly when Julie came along.

For Raye, though, the hard times had started even before that because when we were in New Zealand she helped me to save up so that we could afford to come to England.

Instead of spending our money on going to dances or the pictures we would put it into the savings bank so that we would be able to come over. I suppose we must have really started planning for our first English trip while we were both still at school and only fifteen.

By the time we were ready to come, Raye was a bit keen on the speedway lark herself. People have said to me that it must have been a handicap having a wife and a daughter when I was so young and trying to break into the game thousands of miles away from home.

It was a handicap – a financial handicap inasmuch as when I was in England I had to stick to Wimbledon and couldn't travel elsewhere for rides to perhaps a track where I may have got into a team.

But that was the only handicap because all the time when everyone was telling me that I was never going to be a speedway rider (and when I was beginning to think something like that myself) Raye was the only one who ever believed in me and kept saying that I was going to make it.

Everyone needs someone to give them the encouragement to keep at it and Raye was always there to give me that encouragement. I definitely don't look on it as a handicap. And had it not been for Raye and those true friends we made in the first six months in England I am quite certain that I would have caught the first boat back to Christchurch when the 1957 season ended.

It had hardly been a story-book opening. The teenager who was to be another Ronnie Moore had finished his first season with just three appearances for Wimbledon – and less than half a dozen other meetings at the Southern non-league tracks. Add two meetings in the North and four in Holland and that was the sum total of my 1957 career other than the handful of second half outings at Plough Lane.

Despite this, though, we decided to spend the winter in Wimbledon and looked forward to a future that had to be a lot brighter than the present.

I still had some faith in my own ability – largely sustained by my wife's gentle coaxing and the encouragement of my friends – and felt that I would do a lot better in 1958.

Spending the first Christmas away from home made me realise just how far away New Zealand was and while we thoroughly enjoyed celebrating with our new-found friends, Raye and I couldn't help wonder what the future held for the Mauger family now that there were three mouths to feed.

To make ends meet during the winter I took a variety of jobs, including a few months as a milkman, while Raye worked when she could.

Since I returned to England in 1963 Wimbledon has always claimed a lot of the credit for my progress. It was true I was a junior on their books but frankly the number of rides I was given at Plough Lane could have done little to enhance my progress.

Take my second season, 1958. In the first month of the new season

I had five second half rides at Wimbledon. Between 6th May and 24th August I had another six!

Not all the fault of Ronnie Greene, though, for the Dons – and their supporters – went through a terrifying two months spell when a bus strike in London paralysed public transport and forced the Wimbledon management to close down for the entire month of May and the first three weeks of June. The backlog of fixtures meant that World Championship and international meetings had to be slotted into the programme and in an eleven week spell I had only two after the interval spins! Hardly the encouragement needed if I was to make it to the top.

Fortunately, though, Wimbledon agreed to loan me out to Eastbourne, at that time operating on a non-league Sunday afternoon licence with ex-Don Charlie Dugard at the reins.

The weekly or fortnightly trips from Morden to Arlington became a pleasant break from the bleak scene at Wimbledon. After signing for the Eagles I wore their colours in a challenge match against Chiswick Nomads on Sunday, 8th June and picked up eight points, paid eleven, as well as winning the reserves' race.

I immediately took to the 342-yard Arlington circuit and from then on I had my best run in England. In the next four challenge matches I scored 11, 9, 11 (paid 12) and 12 as well as winning the second half heats and final in every single meeting.

Besides this I won the second half final in a special Olde Tyme meeting and won both the Silver Helmet and Supporters Clubs trophies at Arlington.

At last I was beginning to feel I was getting somewhere but it seemed that no matter what I did at Eastbourne I couldn't get any further at Wimbledon.

My only real chance of being given a continued run as a member of the Dons team was in the National Trophy which, unlike the league, was for ten-man teams.

I must get into Wimbledon's top ten, I thought. And I did – but we lost our first round home-and-away meeting with Norwich so that was the end of that.

A special ten-man challenge at Southampton gave me another ride but other than that my only other team appearance for the Dons was a National League match against Oxford when I fell first time out.

What annoyed me about it was that I was regularly beating

another team member in the limited second half races I was given. At one time Wimbledon announced a great new scheme to help the juniors and put on two heats and a final for the novice. The only problem was that I was considered too good – and missed out on those races too! So there I was – between the Devil and the Deep Blue Sea. I wasn't good enough for a team place. And I was too good for races against other novices.

I've counted the number of rides I actually had at the finely constructed Wimbledon Stadium during 1958 and it comes to . . . 19!

Many youngsters can get that in a month's racing in today's British League!

I wasn't too unhappy though because at least I was having regular rides at Eastbourne. And while the money I earned there didn't do too much towards paying the rent at least I was improving.

Charlie Dugard staged a special test match between a Young England and Young Overseas side – won by Young England – but I got a lot of personal satisfaction by scoring 11 points from the four races I finished. I fell off once and had a troublesome magneto in the other or I may have picked up another five points.

Consolation was that I was the only rider to beat England top scorer Colin Goody who, besides being my team-mate at Eastbourne, also challenged me for top ranking among the junior non-league centres.

The return of Ronnie Moore to Wimbledon did little to convince me that I would be given a chance in the team. With Ronnie back in the line-up I dropped a further place away from a team spot and I began wondering if I wouldn't be better off at another track.

I knew that if I had been able to go somewhere else I would have at least been given an extended run to see if I could make the National League grade. But Wimbledon held my contract – and that was that.

By the end of the season I'd ridden a dozen meetings at Eastbourne and in my last meeting there – the Supporters Club Trophy – I equalled the track record so at least I left England with something in the record book.

As the season wore on I made up my mind that I would return to New Zealand. Money was short and it was becoming increasingly difficult to keep a wife and baby in anything like a decent home.

Raye and I decided there was only one thing to do – send her home by boat before the season ended. Fortunately we had the return ticket for Raye and the money for Julie and she left midway through the season.

It was during the next month or two that I realised how much I relied on her . . . and what a good wife she was. I became more and more tired of trying to make it on my own and once the season was over I told Mr Greene that I was heading back for Christchurch.

And I made it quite clear that if anyone wanted me back in 1959 they would have to find the money to bring my wife as well. It wasn't that I believed I was that good . . . it was just that I would rather forget about English speedway than to be separated from my wife and family.

And ever since then I've made it my duty to ensure that if I go anywhere Raye comes with me.

As in 1957 I was asked by Phil Bishop if I would join his party going over to Holland for the annual Golden Helmet four-meeting series.

This time the party was a bit bigger than the previous season and included South African Trevor Blokdyk, who later gave up speedway to concentrate on a successful car-racing career halted only by a serious injury; tubby Herefordshire man Ray Harris, Pete Lansdale, now a successful promoter and at one time the oldest man riding regular league speedway; Australian Noel Conway; Bill Osborne; another South African Pat McKenzie; and veteran Geoff Pymar. And of course The King of Crash himself.

Again it was an eventful trip – I don't believe any trip with Phil in charge has been anything but – and even though the racing didn't go as well as I might have hoped it was an unforgettable week.

Ray Harris and I tangled up in our first race in the second meeting at Tilburg and neither of us took any further part in that meeting. Earlier I had blown my engine at Den Bosch and had borrowed Phil's to ride in the Tilburg meeting. In the final two meetings I scored a few points but nothing to write home about.

But it is not the racing that has stuck in the memory. Oh no. It was the trip back. Phil, Geoff Pymar, Trevor Blokdyk and myself were all in Phil's Opel Kapital car driving back from Amsterdam to The Hague. With Phil at the wheel we covered the first 115 or so of the 125-mile journey in 1½ hours which gives some idea of the speed at which we were travelling.

But that wasn't fast enough for Phil, truly one of speedway's greatest characters. About ten miles outside The Hague he spotted another car thrashing along at about eighty in the inside lane and decided he would show it a thing or two.

Phil put his foot down and the needle creeped over 80 . . . 85 . . . to 90. He had pulled out into the second lane and was just about level with his adversary when there was a dreadful noise from the engine. We went into a skid as the engine stopped dead. It had blown up. Miraculously Phil kept control and pulled up without any danger to his passengers.

The other car, meanwhile, seeing our plight, had pulled up some distance ahead and the driver slowly reversed back towards us. We all expected a stand-up fight . . . instead the driver was laughing his head off. And towed us the next 10 miles into The Hague where the damage was repaired and we were ready for home.

It isn't generally known that 1958 was also the year I made my World Championship debut! Being Wimbledon's official number eight I was drawn to have two championship rounds – at Ipswich and Coventry.

I went to Ipswich and saw the track for the first time in my life and picked up three points. It might have been more but for a spate of mechanical troubles – something which was holding me back at the time.

A couple of days later I had my second round at Coventry. My successes at Eastbourne had given me some confidence to have a go at the big boys and I was determined to show the Wimbledon management that they were wrong to ignore me the way they had done.

Everything felt right and I went out with only one intention . . . to upset the applecart and score as many points as I could. It was a nerve-wrecking occasion when I looked around the sunken pits at Brandon and saw the big names around me.

There was my boyhood hero, the legendary Jack Young who had won two World Championships. There was quiet-spoken Scotsman Ken McKinlay. There was that great Yorkshireman Arthur Forrest, one of the few top class bespectacled riders of world class. And there was the nervous, green kid Ivan Mauger.

In my first race I had Ron Mountford, Maurie Mattingley and Eric Hockaday. I got a second place which gave me the confidence for my later races. I finished third in my second race and then won my first ever World Championship heat in front of Bryan Elliott, who later emigrated to Australia; Reg Trott, who is still riding at

Eastbourne but who was with Norwich in those days; and one of Birmingham's most popular riders Harry Bastable.

A couple of heats later I knew what the World Championship was all about. For I was lined up against Young . . . McKinlay . . . and Forrest. All in the one heat.

All three were unbeaten up until then – their last ride and I knew that whoever won the race would win the round. I knew I wouldn't win it – but by God I do my darndest to try!

I got out of the gate in front of Hurri-Ken and even though he passed me it was a wonderful experience. Arthur Forrest dropped out of the race so I got myself a point – but more important I'd actually mixed it with Youngie, Mac and Arthur. Until then I'd only admired them from the discomfort but safety of the pits.

Those nine points at Coventry gave me a dozen in my two rounds and while it wasn't good enough to get me any further it was more than two of the riders who were keeping me out of the Wimbledon team.

It may sound as if I felt those two years at Wimbledon were completely wasted. From a riding point of view that may have been the case – but I learnt a lot.

The Brine brothers – Cyril was in the Dons team and Ted was team manager – went out of their way to offer me advice and help, and just by listening and watching my speedway knowledge increased.

Ken Vale and Gil Goldfinch, even though only juniors themselves, also tried to help me whenever they could and what I learned in the pits at Wimbledon every Monday night could fill a book.

When I could I would travel around with Barry Briggs helping him to dope and oil (putting in his fuel and oil) and just by keeping an eye and listening to Barry I learnt far more than I could have done in half a dozen races.

I hadn't really known why a different gear ratio was needed for a different track but I started to pick it up by watching Barry. Besides teaching me what to do he also inadvertently taught me what NOT to do. I remember a meeting at, I think, Leicester. A big individual meeting. Barry won his first couple of races and was way ahead of anyone else. But he wasn't happy and felt he could get into the first bend better if he changed his clutch plates. He changed them – and missed the next two gates! As it happened he charged through in the end but since then I've always left well alone.

If in a World Final I'd won a race I don't think I'd change anything.

At least not unless it was blatantly obvious that something had been wrong.

So even though I didn't get quite as many rides as I would have wished I did learn an awful lot during two seasons at Wimbledon and it was a far from wasted period in my career.

But looking back I am now convinced I would have been better off if I had gone to another track. Instead of trying to emulate Ronnie Moore and Barry Briggs I should have joined a less glamorous set-up than Wimbledon and if I had I might not have spent five years in the Australian wilderness before coming back to England.

When I look back on those times and think of some of the boys I was racing against and beating I realise that if I had stuck it out during the late fifties I would have been a regular team-member within a season or two.

Maybe I wouldn't have been one of the top stars – but I know I could have earnt a living. But that is all water under the bridge now and I have no regrets about the decision I made not to return to England. And no regrets about the decision to spend two seasons in South West London.

Okay, it might have turned out differently if I'd gone elsewhere but I honestly think the tough time I had at the beginning gave something to my character. Something that has stood me in good stead ever since.

It would be wrong to call my trip a complete disaster. I wasn't a top star in the big league. But I was certainly a big fish in a smaller pool and many of the speedway experts rated me the number one man in the Southern Area League conglomeration.

That, I considered, wasn't too bad for an 18-year-old rookie!

4

Let's Start Again

My first trip to England had hardly pleased my bank manager and at times I had often wondered if I would ever make the grade.

Throughout it all my wife Raye had been right behind me and at times she was the only person in the world who had the faith in my ability to make it.

Everyone needs someone offering the right kind of encouragement and for me that person was Raye, even though she suffered terrible hardships herself.

Now, when I look back on my first couple of seasons in England, I believe that I was riding well enough in England in 1958 to warrant coming back again in 1959 but we were really so fed up by this time that we did go home. I was more than a bit disillusioned with England; in particular at the end of 1958 things looked pretty grim in England.

Speedway appeared to be at a very low ebb with only ten teams operating in the league system. We had the money to get back home to New Zealand so we decided that we should make the trip and say goodbye to an English speedway career.

Besides, we didn't really have enough money for the entire family to come back to England and even though I had the money for my own fare I wouldn't have come alone.

I realised that I needed my wife and family with me if I was ever to do well. I did write to one or two promoters in England to see if they would be prepared to bring me over again but I never even had a reply from them so I decided that there was only one thing to do – settle down in New Zealand and buy a house.

Back in New Zealand I was still very much an unknown name so there were no guarantees when I went back to my local Christchurch track at Aranui.

Raye and I decided the first thing we must do was to save up enough money to buy ourselves a house and we had our hearts firmly set on a cottage type of house in Rockinghorse Road, Christchurch. But we didn't have the money so I set to at two jobs.

Before I had gone to England for the first time I had worked as a hosiery presser in a local company and they welcomed me back. Working during the week in that nylon stocking process plant and doing another job as a die caster began to look worthwhile.

Raye had a job in the summer and eventually we had enough money for the deposit on the house in Rockinghorse Road. The little bit extra that I earned from riding at Aranui came in useful and I managed to combine the two jobs and Saturday evening meetings at the local track.

It was quite a big night down at Aranui particularly when my heroes Ronnie Moore, Barry Briggs, Geoff Mardon and Trevor Redmond were riding.

Those early days at Aranui as a teenager have stood me in good stead since and it must be hard for anyone in England to realise that four World class stars like Moore, Mardon, Briggs and Redmond would ride at a very small track in Christchurch.

Today all but Geoff Mardon are still actively engaged in speedway. Ronnie and Barry are, of course, still riding in the British League and both of them reached last year's World Final even though Ronnie had to be content with the reserve berth following an unfortunate accident in the European Final in Leningrad.

Trevor, after a spell out of speedway, came back in 1970 as co-promoter at Wembley and also acted as team manager to the New Zealand Test team.

Geoff, who many rated on a par with the other three, announced a premature retirement from the sport and hasn't been seen on the track for some years now. But he still has quite an interest in the sport back in Christchurch.

At the tender age of 19 Raye and I decided to retire from the world travelling and thought that we would happily settle down in our house in Christchurch.

We paid the deposit . . . moved in . . . began to build up the furniture; speedway outside New Zealand was a long way from my mind. The local scene wasn't quite what it had been as the Aranui track had to close down so that the site could be re-developed for a new school.

Ironic, I suppose, that a track that had provided so much entertainment for the schoolchildren of Christchurch should have to close its doors so that it could be turned into classrooms! Mind you I would think many a youngster has since dreamed of his leather clad hero sweeping around the bends where his desk has stood.

However we weren't in our house for more than a few weeks when I had a letter from Australian promoter Kym Bonython who was later to become a very good friend.

Once Aranui had closed down I had virtually given up any thoughts of continuing riding outside New Zealand, but I did sit down one afternoon and write a couple of letters to the Australian speedway promoters.

I didn't really think I would get any answers but thought it might make a useful exercise. I remembered what had happened when I wrote off to the promoters in England and didn't think too much more about it all.

Then I had a couple of replies – thanking me for the letter and saying they might look me up in a year or two. But there was nothing to make me think that I'd be spending my next few years commuting between New Zealand and Australia.

Anyway, I had answers from all the Aussie promoters – either saying 'no thanks' or 'we'll call you again next year' – until the letter arrived at Rockinghorse Road from Mr Bonython.

He was promoting at Adelaide and wrote over saying he would pay the fares of Raye, myself and the family and bikes. That was the beginning of my first taste of racing in Australia.

At that time I had done fairly well or so I thought – in New Zealand.

While I was far from being a really big name in my own country I felt that at 19 I had achieved some considerable success.

After all, I thought to myself, if I am good enough to finish second to Barry Briggs in the New Zealand Championship, I must be ready for the trip to Australia.

The Speedway Family Mauger. *Left to right:* Debbie, Dad Ivan, Kym, Mum Raye and Julie

At one time hockey was the game for me. I captained the school 'C' grade team back in 1953. That's me holding the hockey sticks

As a teenager I had a few rides for Southern Area League Eastbourne. Here I'm in Eastbourne's colours in 1958

Wimbledon practice, Easter, 1957. Rookie Ivan Mauger wears the Wimbledon body-colour for the first time

A photograph taken before my unsuccessful attack on the Australian Long-Track Championship at Port Pirie, Easter, 1960. I won the title eventually, however

5

Riding Around Aussie —on a Junk Heap!

The thought of riding in Australia filled me with hope.

Even though my first trip to England had been far from what I had hoped – or expected – I still had enough faith in my own ability to chance my arm again.

It was in October or November, 1959, that we were to go to Adelaide for the first time – in fact I was to have four successive seasons there.

The first Adelaide season I rode quite well and was happy with my riding. But while I was riding well I couldn't say that my bikes were what they should have been.

I had all kinds of mechanics working on the bikes but no matter how long they spent on the engines I seemed to be plagued by engine failure after engine failure.

I put up one or two good performances against the top Australians but every time it came to the crunch I found myself having to pull out of a race.

Kym Bonython, who was to become a very great friend, helped me through this patch and never complained that he had brought me over and I wasn't going as well as I should.

Kym is probably one of the great characters in speedway for besides promoting the sport he was also one of Australia's best known art connoisseurs. He ran a couple of art galleries and every public library in Australia contained at least one of his books on art. He also ran a local television programme, so was quite a big personality in his own right outside speedway.

After my first year in Australia I returned to New Zealand with Raye quite convinced that my speedway career was over as far as riding outside New Zealand was concerned. I'd been to England and failed to make the senior grade. And I'd been to Australia and turned in too many disappointing performances!

In the winter I wrote to Kym again and said that I would like to have another go and see if I could make up for some of my less bright shows during the winter of 1959.

I must say that Kym was the first promoter to pay any real interest in me and I was pleasantly surprised when he replied and invited me back.

He not only said he wanted me back at Adelaide – but he also offered me exactly the same terms as the season before, when I had been expecting him to say he didn't want me that season at all!

He did, however, lay down one stipulation – I must buy a new bike. He offered, because I think he realised I didn't have a lot of money, to buy a brand new Jap engine on condition that I supplied a first class frame to put it in.

This was, in fact, the first piece of brand new equipment that I had ever had and also started off an association with Fred Jolly who was at that time the Adelaide Jap importer.

It was a custom of Fred to buy bikes off the top English boys and the year before Alf Hagon had been out in Aussie and had sold Fred a fairly good machine. I'd often admired the Rotrax when I had been out at Fred's the year before, and wrote over to ask if I could buy it off him.

Again I got a surprise when the reply popped through the letter box, because Fred offered to lend me the complete bike less engine for the season because it was from him that Kym was buying me the new engine.

I think that, like Kym, Fred realised I didn't have much money and I couldn't have afforded to buy that bike off him. As with Kym I'll be forever grateful to Fred for what he did for me in those days.

Kym did make one other stipulation – that Jock Grierson, the former Hastings and Coventry rider who was, at that time, living in Adelaide, was to do the engine and I wasn't to touch it.

It appeared to me that while Kym had a lot of faith in my ability as a rider he didn't think too much about my abilities as a mechanic! This didn't bother me though, because I was up in the clouds because a promoter was going to take me from New Zealand to Australia – with my family. And he was going to buy me a new engine at the same time.

I was very grateful to Kym and happy that when I went back at the end of 1960 I won just about everything there was to win in those days on the Adelaide track.

Jock Grierson took my engines in charge as he had done during the last few weeks of the previous season when I had been riding for Kym at Rowley Park.

Jock had built himself up a big reputation among the Adelaide riders as an engine tuner and most of the top-class riders went along to him. It was his reputation that convinced me I would be better off with him looking after my engines because, up until then, I had been doing it myself when I hadn't really got a wide enough knowledge of what to do.

Even now I can remember going into Jock's shop in Adelaide for the first time and him saying something to the effect 'I've been watching you all season and you can ride okay – but your bikes have been a bit junky!'

During that last week or so in Adelaide during 1960 I had some very good meetings so when Kym said Jock had to look after the engines the following year I readily agreed.

I realised then that no one would ever make it to the top unless they were mounted on really good class equipment.

The Adelaide season starts on the first Friday of November every year and I was ready for the first meeting of the 1960-61 season. While in Adelaide I always augmented my speedway earnings by driving trucks for a firm who employed me every year I went across. This enabled me to keep my head above water.

The 1960-61 season proved to be a very good season for me – I never had one engine failure and ended up equalling Ken McKinlay's track record which had stood for many years.

Early in 1961 Fred Jolly started talking to me about a new Czechoslovakian bike called an Eso and he showed me photographs that he had received from behind the Iron Curtain.

I thought then that it looked a dream and Fred told me he was having one sent over which would arrive in Australia early in 1961 in time for Ove Fundin to ride it in the South Australian Championship.

The bike duly arrived and predictably Ove rode it into first place with Aub Lawson second and myself third. Then Fred said I could ride it in the Australian Long-Track Championship at Port Pirie – a one-mile speedway track – in the Easter meeting.

Traditionally the meeting is held on Easter Saturday and the previous year I was leading after four of the five laps when the engine seized.

So I was eager to try and get the title I thought I should have won 12 months previously. Fred wouldn't let me ride the Eso during the remaining meetings at Rowley Park in case anything went wrong with the engine because he wasn't in a position then to get parts out to Australia from Czechoslovakia in a matter of days or even weeks.

Fred was anxious to win the long-track title in order to promote sales for the Eso and wouldn't risk something going wrong with the machine before the championship came round.

As you can imagine in the weeks before Easter I was jumping around like a cat on a hot tin roof just itching to have a ride on the thing.

Practice is traditionally Good Friday with the race the following day and on the Friday we had some minor troubles with the engine which stopped me from having more than a lap or two in practice.

We worked on the bike all Friday night and the club bent the rules a bit and allowed me to have a couple of laps of practice on the Saturday morning – laps that went fairly well and gave me an opportunity to learn a little more about the bike for the meeting.

It was obvious that the bike was going because in my first heat I took over eleven seconds off the existing record which had been held by the late Gerry Hussey.

I went to the starting line in the final really confident of winning a big championship and after about four laps I was about half a mile in the lead and going away when the clutch came off.

On the early Esos the clutch was on a taper and it was never really very good. It was this fundamental fault in design that lost me another chance of winning the long-track title.

All wasn't lost, however, as I did have the track record. This was something that Fred could advertise so things were beginning to look promising for Eso in Australia.

He had also promised that I could have a new Eso in the following Adelaide season for which Kym Bonython had already offered me a slight rise over the terms I had agreed for the 1960-61 spell.

Not only were things starting to look up for the Eso in Australia speedway but things were also starting to look up for Ivan Mauger. Because of this I decided to stay in Adelaide that Aussie winter (1961) instead of going back to Christchurch, in order that I could prepare things and really be in line for when the season started.

I decided to have an all-out attack on getting started from the very first meeting. At the same time a friend of mine in Adelaide, Bob Timms, had offered to buy a Greeves for me to ride in the Moto-Cross series around Australia that winter.

I was quite interested to do this and together – Bob as the owner and tuner and me as the rider – we won a few championships at club level.

This didn't, however, stop me thinking about the speedway season starting the following October – and the new Eso that was arriving for me to use.

Speedway was going quite well up in Rockhampton and Townsville in North Queensland but it seemed to be too far for me to go, particularly as, being a family man, there wasn't enough money for me to spend the entire season at Rocky.

However, in the September of 1961 the Rockhampton promoter phoned me and asked if I would go up there and do two meetings at Rocky and two at Townsville.

The first at Rocky would be the Australian Championship for 1961 and this time all I had was my Jap engine, that Kym had bought me the season before, and the Rotrax that Fred had given me. I was still eagerly awaiting the arrival of the Eso.

I managed to borrow a bike off a friend in Adelaide, put my engine in it and went off to Queensland for the four meetings. I drove day-and-night without stopping to make sure I got there in time for the meeting.

In the championship I got second to Bob Sharp and in the other meeting won most events until I blew the engine up in my last meeting. This didn't worry me too much though, because all I was concerned about was getting back to my family who had stayed in Adelaide and I was anticipating seeing the brand new Eso waiting for me in Fred's showrooms.

So I was a bit disappointed to hear that the ship was about three weeks behind schedule and I had to ride another borrowed Jap for the first three meetings.

Eventually the Eso arrived in time for what was the fourth meeting of the Adelaide season and I cleaned up on it in a big way for practically the entire season except for one night when I dropped a valve in it.

I also won the Victorian Championship in February, 1962, when

Jack Young and I drove the 500 or so miles from Adelaide to Melbourne for the championship.

Jack got second in the meeting which made me very proud, for it was not only my first really major championship win but it was also an honour to beat Youngie, a man whom I had admired ever since I first learnt anything about speedway.

There were still a few meetings left at Adelaide after the Victorian Championship but my main thoughts were the Easter Saturday Long-Track Championship at Port Pirie.

Bearing in mind what had happened to me the two previous years we – Jock Grierson, Fred Jolly and myself – really went to the extremes to check the bike over to try and ensure I didn't have engine failure again. We had the tapers checked to make sure the clutch wouldn't come off the shaft again, and generally inspected the engine to make sure it was mechanically perfect.

We went up and everything seemed to go pretty well at practice on the Friday. At this time Jack Scott hadn't been back long from England. He had had a big win on the pools and was reputed to have an ultra-fast Jap engine.

Unofficial times gave me a few seconds advantage over Scotty so I was quite confident when it came to the final.

In the heats on the Saturday my times weren't much faster than Scotty's but because of what had happened the two previous years I was riding with a good deal of reserve and I honestly believe Scotty was going all out.

I knew that I was a good five or ten seconds faster than him in the heats, particularly as I had something in reserve. Between the heats and final I raised the gearing one tooth on the back sprocket in order that I could hold bottom gear just that little bit longer because I was frightened that the Jap would outpull the Eso to the first bend and I didn't what to have to change gear too early.

By going higher it gave me a better chance of getting into the bend first because that is particularly important on the long track where the shale hits you so hard that it can just about wipe you off the bike.

I made a very good start but when I changed gear Scotty's Jap pulled up alongside me! However, when I built up the revs I pulled away and won it reasonably comfortably that year.

In fact I really learnt a lot that was to stand me in good stead in later years from that victory. I would be about 100 yards ahead of

Scotty and would let him get up to 90 yards and then I would turn the throttle and pull out to about 110 yards and then knock it back again a little so that I was always between 90 and 110 yards in front of him.

In many championship events later on I was to use this technique because I learnt that it isn't necessary to keep the throttle full on from the start to the finish of a race. That is the mistake I had made in the long-track event for two years and I wasn't going to do it again.

I think it was that period of my career which taught me to ride to win and not necessarily ride to go fast. Since then, that has always been my policy and it has brought its rewards – not in track records but in victories.

It was now Easter 1962 and the contacts I had made the previous October with Rockhampton promoter Ted Price resulted in him asking if I would spend the winter of '62 (Australia's winter – England's summer) at his track.

I had told him that I would join him for the season providing I wasn't returning to England. I did feel that I could make it again in Britain and had written to quite a number of the English promoters asking if they would bring me over. Again I never received any replies so with the family, which had now grown to my wife Raye and three children – Julie, the eldest, Kym who had been born in Christchurch on 1st November, 1959, and Debbie who was born in Adelaide on 5th May the previous year – I headed for Rockhampton which meant a trip of just over 2,000 miles through Australia's outback.

Now, when I think of all the things that have happened to me in speedway, this trip is just one of the many adventures we have had. On it you can drive for something like 250 miles without seeing a house or any living animal at all.

There is a sign at the beginning of the highways saying you must take oil, food and so on with you because of the lack of facilities. We really all thought we were on safari and for long stretches it was hard to believe that we would ever see civilisation again.

On the back of the Vanguard car I had at the time, we had a trailer with my Eso bike and all the other bits and pieces that we would need in Rockhampton.

We must certainly have made an amusing sight as a family with three children all under school age trekked across the outback towing a trailer with a gleaming chrome bike and all sorts of personal things such as pots, pans and our clothes.

Eventually we arrived at Rockhampton on the Friday after spending a couple of days driving across the desert. During our trip we realised how the explorers who first discovered America must have felt as they covered miles and miles of country without seeing life.

I had another good season at Rocky and I also rode at Mackay every second week. I won the Queensland Championship the second week I was at Rockhampton so that was my third big championship in Australian speedway . . . and luckily all within about three months.

I really think the spell I had at Rockhampton from Easter '62 until the end of the season in October provided me and the family with some of the best times we have ever had from speedway.

As I've already mentioned, the children were too young to go to school and I didn't work, mainly because it was a small town with only a few thousand population and there weren't any jobs around. I was only riding speedway every second Saturday night.

We were down at the Olympic-sized swimming pool a lot . . . had drives out into the beautiful countryside . . . had visits to beaches . . . picnics every day. A really good time.

I had also by then learnt a bit about the Eso and there were one or two Eso's at odd places in Australia at the time and I was doing a bit of work on engines for the Queensland riders. It not only earned me a few quid but also gave me more and more experience of what made an engine tick.

I suppose it was somewhat ironic that a rider who had originally been warned not to touch his own engine should now be looking after those belonging to other boys but by then I had learnt a lot more about the mechanical side of speedway than I had known a few years earlier.

When the Rockhampton season ended in October it was time to start the long drive back to Adelaide for their November opener. We had planned to take a month on the drive so that we could have a really good holiday on the way back and I was going to do three meetings – one at Brisbane, one at Sydney and one at Melbourne. It meant we could drive leisurely down to Brisbane and again down to Sydney stopping on the way at any town we might like the look of.

At the last minute the Melbourne meeting was cancelled and the Brisbane promoter booked me in for two meetings. However the first was rained out and I ended up doing only one meeting at Brisbane, one at Sydney and then across to Adelaide. Those two meetings were in four weeks so we were able to spend our time on the trip and to this day that year remains as one of the most satisfying I have ever spent – not from a financial angle but from enjoying speedway.

While we had a ball and lots of fun I still had ambitions of coming back to England as a full-time rider and even though it was a carefree time off the track I was dedicated to winning on the track so that I could realise those ambitions.

Once again I had a very good season at Adelaide and for me the crowning glory was when I won the Victorian Championship again, because no one had won it two seasons on the run.

Throughout this time I was posting off letters to the English promoters but, of course, there were never any coming the other way. I was beginning to think that I would never get back to England and even though I kept reading of English promoters being interested in signing Ivan Mauger I began to think that there must have been someone else of the same name because I certainly didn't know anything about it!

It wasn't until Ivan Crozier suggested that I should drop a line to an English promoter by the name of Mike Parker that I got a reply.

And, lo and behold, back came a telegram which arrived in Adelaide the day I was in Melbourne defending the Victorian Championship.

Raye, realising how important it was, had it re-directed across to Melbourne where I received it in the pits just before the meeting. In my letter to Mike I said that to come to England I'd have to have the fares for my family and myself – just as I'd written to virtually every other English promoter.

The telegram read simply: 'Fares paid, Cooks Manchester. Tickets at Cooks Adelaide.'

That was that and virtually the finish of my Australian career as far as being a resident Australian rider . . . and the start of my English career.

I've had many further experiences of Australia but only on short touring trips.

It is only now when I look back at the seasons I spent in Australia that I realise how vital those years were on the pathway to the World title.

Thrown together and bound neatly with a piece of string they may seem very little. But I have no doubt that I laid the foundation on which to build during the long hot summers in Adelaide.

Even now I find it impossible accurately to assess the value of speedway Down Under but I know that without it I may never have been World Champion.

As a footballer remembers his years in the reserves and junior sides as the time when his style and his future was fashioned, so I look upon Australia as the mould out of which was poured a World speedway champion.

Adelaide was always a Friday night – most tracks in Australasia are a Saturday night – and because of this I was able to travel from Adelaide 500 miles across country to Melbourne with Jack Young to compete in meetings on the Saturday night.

Once we even drove 1,000 miles across to Sydney to ride in one of their Saturday night meetings. It wasn't so much the experience of riding in Melbourne or Sydney that proved to be beneficial in later years. As much as that was the actual experience of driving such distances!

Now when I travel so much to the Continent and can ride in different countries every day of the week, the Australian grounding I had has been of great benefit to me. Also, talking to Jack Young non-stop on a 500 miles journey helped me because I got to know a lot about England; how to go about different things; so nearly everything I did on Australian speedway helped me and does help me today.

I also learnt a lot about how to overtake riders because most of the Australian programme is dominated by handicap racing. While this may often appear to be a more dangerous form of racing than the traditional scratch racing in Britain it does at least give you a lot of experience.

To begin with, you start off on the front marker with all the more experienced riders giving you quite a start and this can afford you the confidence to beat a man who is obviously a far better rider than you are.

It can also teach you how to prevent a faster man passing you and probably accelerates the rate of progress because you have a fair chance of gaining experience and winning races early in your career, as opposed to England where the novice always starts off by losing race after race.

As you move back on handicap so it gets harder – and so you

learn more and more about the riders in front of you. Eventually at Adelaide I was as far back as the 240 yard mark on the big Rowley Park track.

In my last meeting at Adelaide, I remember, I was on the back mark, Jack Young was on 220, Ken McKinlay was on 200 yards, Mike Broadbanks on about 190 yards and the effort needed to pass riders like that taught me a great deal about technique and it was then that I began to read a race and plan how to pass someone rather than just try and blast around.

Towards the end of 1962 in Australia I realised that speedway was on the up and up in England and I was keen to come back. In 1961 Jock Grierson had written to Coventry on my behalf saying that he thought I was World class but they apparently never replied to his letter.

In the following year, around about Christmas time, Jock received a telegram from Coventry saying 'We are interested in Mauger – please have him write to us.'

I guess that within five minutes of Jock telling me about the telegram I had written the letter and posted it to them, but once again no reply ever reached me.

That's the way I thought it would be – until the telegram from Mike Parker. . . .

6

Five Boat Tickets . . . and a Second Chance

It had been a peaceful, restful trip across the oceans.

With thousands of miles of water (and ports) behind us – my wife Raye, our children Julie, Debbie, Kym and myself – we slowly sailed into the Southampton harbour a few days before Easter 1963.

I was coming back to England to begin my career. I say begin because that is what I was doing. I had been in England in 1957 and 1958 but as far as I was concerned that was purely to gain experience.

Then I had been a star-struck teenager with very little knowledge of the speedway world, let alone the outside world. I had barely been out of my hometown Christchurch, never mind trying to make my way in the hardest speedway league in the world.

But by the time I docked at Southampton that was all at the back of my mind. I don't know what I had expected but everything seemed different as we moored at the dockside.

I knew that this was the beginning of my real speedway career. I was arriving in England with just one intention – to ride speedway and nothing else. If I was to have anything to do with it I would be a full-time rider . . . and wouldn't need a part-time job to keep myself and the family.

All kinds of thoughts meandered through my mind on the six-week crossing on the *Castle Felice*. Would I be good enough? Had British speedway changed? How high was the standard of the Provincial League? These and a hundred or more such hypothetical questions filled my mind during those seemingly endless thirty odd days between sailing out of New Zealand and broaching the English channel.

We quickly docked, disembarked and got through customs. On the quayside was a man who was to take care of us for the next couple of years . . . Eddie Glennon.

Eddie, at that time right-hand man to promoter Mike Parker and later a co-promoter with Mike in his own right, was tragically killed in a car accident some years later.

Eddie had us pile into his car and swiftly he drove from Southampton through the heart of what was still a strange and unfamiliar country to Manchester.

As I had never been to Belle Vue before it was the first time that I had visited the northern city. I remember thinking how drab it looked. Later I was to become attached to Manchester – an attachment that grew into a fondness for the city and its people. So much so that since that first day back we have always lived in or around Manchester.

Eddie took us into Mike Parker's offices which were then in Moss Lane and we met the man who was to be my employer for the next five years.

Mike had a bike there for me to ride and even though it was something of a junkie thing, it was enough to get me through those first few matches over the Easter week-end.

I had four days grace before I was ready for my first English meeting in nearly six years. I'd missed Newcastle's opening away meeting at Edinburgh but was in time for the 'derby' Northern League match at Middlesbrough on Thursday, 11th April.

As I drove up to Middlesbrough I wondered what would greet me. On my first visit I had ridden exclusively in the National and Southern Area League. One was very much the well-established higher echelon of league racing – the other more a training ground,

During my first couple of days I'd met a few riders – and most of them had told me how I would notice a change. Instead of the ultra-slick and smooth tracks of the 1958 days I would find things a lot rougher.

I was more than apprehensive as I slipped out of my clothes into leathers for my opening meeting. I'd been given something of a big build-up in the speedway press and the local papers in Newcastle, and was a little worried as to whether I would live up to the advance publicity. The fact that I was on a machine I had never ridden before did little to rid me of my anxieties.

But now for the crunch – the testing moment. I was number four in the Diamonds side which, in those days meant I came out in the second heat. A touch of sympathetic team managership had seen that I was partnered with another New Zealander – Ivan Crozier.

We had been friends and it was something to go on parade with a familiar face alongside me. In fact I felt very much at home in that first meeting because another team-mate was fellow countryman Bob Duckworth.

The weather was foul – there was no other way to describe it – I was certain that the meeting would never start. The track was in an atrocious state, sticky, slimy and altogether the opposite of what I had been used to in Australia.

A number of the boys were a little undecided about whether they should ride or not but in the end we decided that it would have been unfair on those fans who had paid to get in if we pulled out.

It wasn't a happy Provincial League debut. I took a tumble in one race (escaped shaken but unbowed) and had problems with wet magnetos and soaked clutches and ended up with just two points to my name.

Not an overwhelming sensation – but in myself I felt happy enough. I knew that given a good bike and a bit of luck I could hold my own in the team.

What made me even more confident was the fact that I wasn't the only Diamond to have a rough time. Even our skipper Brian Craven – very much a top-liner in those days – had a struggle to pick up half a dozen points. And I knew the track was in a bad state . . . so much so that we all pulled out of the second half.

That was a decision that I didn't have too much say in – unlike others that were to be made in later years. All in all an eventful return.

My main feelings about the first meeting was that things could only get better . . . they certainly couldn't have been much worse.

I knew, though, that I had gone to the meeting completely disorganised. Everything had been done in such a rush. We had sorted out living accommodation, schools for the children and things like that. All of which hadn't left me too much time to think about riding!

The following night Mike Parker had fixed up for me to go down to Wolverhampton for a second half booking. I was to have a series of match races against Tommy Sweetman who was the big star down at Wolverhampton.

On a borrowed bike – not the one I had been using the previous night – I managed to beat Tommy by two races to one in a three match race series.

I also did the fastest time of the night on the 329-yard Wolverhampton track – the first time I had seen the track so that gave me quite a bit more confidence than the night before.

On the Saturday I got down to trying to sort out my engine problems and worked a bit on Thursday's bike and took it up with me to Newcastle for my home debut.

Again I was a little apprehensive and worried about the reception I would get. The speedway press were building me up and everyone was talking about Newcastle's new signing – the ex National League star with mighty Wimbledon.

Too many had forgotten that during my days at Wimbledon I had had so few meetings that I could probably have counted them on the hands of the seven Newcastle riders! And that included second half rides spread over two seasons!

I'd been satisfied with my first away meeting in Newcastle's colours. Now for my first home appearance.

It also happened to be Newcastle's opening match of the new campaign, a challenge match against one of Mike Parker's other promoting concerns, Wolverhampton.

Any thought that I might have had that it would be an easy meeting because both outfits were bossed by the same man were soon dispelled and I realised it was going to be no cake-walk to establish myself in the league.

I had to ride four different bikes on that evening and scored a handful of points. Nothing spectacular but again enough to give me the confidence to know that once I had a good machine under me I could start looking for the points.

But I also knew that until I got a good bike it would be useless my trying to compete on level terms with the rest of the boys.

But this time I'd contacted a few people I had known in 1958 and I heard that Ted Brine had his brother Cyril's bike for sale.

From my Wimbledon days – when we were team-mates – I knew how well Ted had looked after the bike and was confident that this was the bike I needed.

I phoned Ted and went down to London the day after my first meeting at Newcastle and bought the bike for £125 and was still using parts off it up until the day I came off Japs for good about midway through the 1968 British season.

Now that I had got a good bike under me I began to look forward to my next meeting. On my first meeting at Newcastle I had taken an instant shine to the track and felt that I would grow to enjoy it every week.

It had come as quite a surprise to me because in my first five days in England I'd been told what a terrible track it was by practically everyone I met. I'd been told it was rough, bumpy and a horrible place to ride.

I found it rough and I found it bumpy and a funny shape – but I took to it anyway. That was probably just as well as it was to be my home base for the next five years.

The fact that I was back in England and now a full-time speedway rider was all that mattered to me at that time. I didn't mind that a track was rough, or bumpy, or a strange shape. And I didn't even worry if it was raining.

Now that I think about it, I was out of English speedway for five years and those five years undoubtedly held me back but it is impossible to say whether I would have been a World Champion five years earlier.

My determination to be a speedway rider always overcame any of the problems of tracks and it was normal for me always to have to face problems, and in this case bumpy tracks never bothered me.

Even today a bumpy or a wet track doesn't bother me at all. It doesn't however mean that I am condoning the condition of half of the tracks in the British League, but that is something that I will be dealing with later.

With Cyril Brine's old bike as my regular mount I was ready for my second away match – this time another Northern League clash with Sheffield.

I ended that meeting with my best score so far – nine points – but it is not for this reason that I will remember my first trip to Owlerton.

The meeting was marred by a tragic accident that ended the racing career of one of the top men in the Provincial League – Sheffield captain Guy Allott – even before the tapes went up on the first heat.

In those days Sheffield had a tradition that the team would make a tractor parade before the meeting started and poor Guy fell from the tractor and was rushed to hospital with serious head, neck and arm injuries.

It cast a dreadful pall on the meeting but I am glad to say that

It hasn't all been fun and games. The 1965 World Championship round at Glasgow, for example, saw me lifted on and off my bike. Notice the special casing around my left foot, protecting a broken ankle

The Newcastle Supporters' Club present Raye and myself with a scroll on behalf of my team-mates, managers and supporters, in recognition of my efforts in 1965 British season despite injuries

Racing around the world. Here I am untroubled and leading in a German international meeting

Guy later recovered and while he never returned to his track-blazing career he became acknowledged as one of the finest engine tuners in the country.

I was to develop a strong and close relationship with Guy in later years and Guy was the man who prepared my engines for my three final wins.

My first ever British maximum came, predictably enough, at Brough Park, in what was my sixth match for the Diamonds against Middlesbrough in the last of our Northern League encounters on Monday, May 13th.

Certainly not a case of thirteen being unlucky – and a date that meant a lot to me because I had proved to myself that I had been right to come back to England to start all over again.

At last I was really finding my way around the British tracks and with Newcastle skipper Brian Craven also in fine form we were beginning to make a challenge at the top of the Provincial League table.

While we were struggling to win away we strung together an impressive row of home wins with Brian and myself viewing at the top of the scorers list.

So confident was Mike Parker of our ability as a pairing that he booked in the Belle Vue pair Dick Fisher and Dent Oliver for a special match race at Brough Park.

In those days Belle Vue were very much the elite, being in what was the equivalent of speedway's First Division while we were in the Second. But most critics felt that the gap separating the two divisions was as yawning as the Grand Canyon.

Fortunately we managed to preserve the dignity of the Provincial League by coming out on top in a best-of-three series. Another fillip to the lower division was a special 'test' match series against what was labelled a National League 'B' side.

I was picked for most of the matches and managed to do pretty well. All of which made me even more determined to do well in the World Championship rounds.

I'd had a couple of meetings during my first trip – by now a distant memory – but hadn't progressed any further than my first round.

Even in 1963 the World Championship was of prime importance and I spent the first week or so of June preparing my bike to make sure it wouldn't let me down.

During league meetings I'd hit a winning streak and five days before my opening World Champion round I had taken the Provincial League individual match-race title – the Silver Sash – from Hackney Wick's leading scorer Norman Hunter on his own track.

I had only two qualifying meetings in 1963 in the first round and drew my own track and Wolverhampton. In fact it couldn't have been better as far as I was concerned.

My first round was at Brough Park on Monday, June 10th and despite dropping a point to that man Brian Craven I won the round with 14 points – Brian having looped at the gate in his first heat.

I went one better at Wolverhampton and ended with a 15 point score from my five rides – enough to make sure that I was one of the 16 lined up for the Provincial Final of the Championship – the last step before we Provincial lads were ready to mix it with the National League boys.

Again I dropped a point, in the final at Edinburgh, but once more 14 points was good enough to win the meeting and take me through to the next round.

There I was drawn at Swindon, Southampton and Oxford – three tracks that I had known during my first visit. I didn't have too happy a time at Swindon and came into my second round needing a good performance if I was to have a chance of getting any further in the championship.

I was drawn number one in the programme which meant a first heat opening. When I looked at the programme there were many names that had meant so much to me.

Belle Vue's brilliant leader Peter Craven . . . seasoned international Cyril Roger . . . internationals Jack Geran and Jimmy Gooch . . . and the New Zealander I knew so much about – Barry Briggs.

What a start I thought as I coasted up to the line for the meeting that would make or break my 1963 championship hopes.

I suppose every rider has it at the back of his mind that he is going to be World Champion one day – and I suppose I was secretly thinking that it would happen to me.

It was – but not in 1963! In my first ride I crashed heavily with Dick Fisher and had a very bad shaking and was quite dizzy and dazed for the rest of the meeting.

Even so I won one race and slipped under the shower with a bad head and five points to my name. Looking back now it is odd how many boys there were in that qualifying round who are still very big names in British speedway. And how many were just starting their career in those days.

Scot George Hunter, Wimbledon's Reg Luckhurst, Briggo, Jimmy Gooch, Cyril Maidment, Martin Ashby and Terry Betts were all in that one qualifying round.

They were the riders who really put me out of the World Championship in 1963.

The World Championship over, it was back to the bread and butter of league competition with a thin spreading of representative matches for such teams as Overseas in a test series against Britain.

Right until the last few meetings Newcastle were in with a chance of taking the league but eventually we had to concede and the title went to Wolverhampton.

On the individual front I was being invited to more and more meetings and particularly in the last few weeks of the season I could be riding practically every evening.

I won quite a lot of these fairly important Provincial League open meetings but the big meeting was still to come – the Provincial League Riders Championship which was the forerunner of today's British League Riders Championship. Then, as now, it was held at Belle Vue.

We all had three qualifying rounds and I went into the final sharing the top qualifying spot with Colin Pratt who was riding for Stoke. We had both scored 43 out of a possible 45 points but I knew that the Belle Vue meeting was far from a two horse race.

There was a somewhat curious formula adopted for the final with 24 riders qualifying to take part. In fact we all had a series of qualifying races with the top four scorers going into a final – the winner of which would be the new champion.

The one big drawback about the formula was that the luck of the draw played a far bigger part in the meeting than is normal for a championship field.

Theoretically – and in practice – it would be possible for a man to win the title without meeting every other rider.

I got off to a good start with a win in heat one but dropped a point in my second ride when I was beaten by Sheffield's Jack Kitchen.

Kitch went through his four qualifying rides unbeaten. I won my last two races and had eleven points. Ross Gilbertson, George Hunter, Clive Featherby, Maurie Mattingley and Ray Cresp all had nine points to fill the remaining two places in the final.

It was Hunter and Gilbertson who clinched the two places for the final run-off . . . but not before an uproar that threatened to end the meeting without a champion being crowned.

The root of the rumpus was the final four run-off. The five riders had tied with nine points each. According to the meeting rule – mentioned in the programme – if there was a tie for any of the four final places it would be decided by the greatest number of heat wins. If this failed riders with the fastest winning times would go forward.

Gilbertson and Hunter had two wins apiece; the other three one each. They should have gone through and, in fact it was announced that they would make up the final with Kitch and myself.

We even got so far as to ride up to the tapes underneath the Belle Vue grandstand ready to start the race. Then I saw Jimmy Squibb on the track holding his steel-shoe. Other riders came out of the pits and poured onto the track in a seemingly never ending stream of discontent.

It soon became obvious that the competitors had got together and decided that it was an unfair way to decide the final four. They were demanding a race-off between the five riders who had tied on points . . . with the first two going into the final.

In my view a reasonable proposition – but then I wasn't one of the five. Certainly the odd way of running the meeting made this the fairest way of selection. After all the riders hadn't met every opponent in the qualifying rounds and it could have been argued that Gilbertson and Hunter – the two with a pair of race wins each – had had easier qualifying races than the other three.

Before the four of us came out on the track I knew that there was trouble. The only two who were happy about the situation were Kitch and myself because no matter how they decided on qualifying the other two we were through into the final.

Much to the disgust of the other competitors the organisers decided to stick to the rules as laid out in the programme and duly put Gilbertson and Hunter in.

However I sensed that this wasn't the end of it and I wasn't really surprised when I saw the rest of the boys walking on the track as we rode up to the tapes.

Jimmy Squibb was the main figure of the incident with his striking eyes, and his dark beard giving him an impressive look as he stood there under the arc-lights with the steel shoe glinting in his hand.

He wasn't intending to use it as a weapon, merely as a prop and we all knew this. The rest of them walked out behind him . . . up to the starting tapes . . . and then their demonstration.

They all laid out across the track at the starting gate making it impossible for the race to begin. Everyone, except the four of us ready to race, were arguing with each other.

Confusion reigned as riders, stewards, promoters and track officials argued to and fro trying to sort it out. One thing was made clear – the riders were determined to see a run-off with ALL five taking part.

And eventually this came about when, ironically, the two who got through were Hunter and Gilbertson! So once again the four of us went up to the line.

This time there were no problems – and the tapes shot up and I chased into the first corner to take the title with Kitch second and Gilby third. Unlucky Georgie Hunter dropped out with engine trouble, while leading.

So I had won my first major non-world championship title in England.

But what very few people knew was that I had done it while I was sick.

I hadn't been feeling well all through the meeting although I didn't find any great strain while I was actually riding. But I knew in between heats that I was nowhere near 100 per cent and my mind often wandered when I wasn't on the track . . . something which was uncharacteristic.

During the general rumpus I was having great difficulty in keeping my mind fully trained on what I had to do and after the meeting I turned up for a celebration laid on by Mike Parker but only stayed a few minutes.

I definitely didn't feel like celebrating which was strange considering I had just won what was the biggest meeting of the Provincial League.

I went home to bed and got up the following day and still didn't feel too good.

Within 12 hours I was in hospital . . . with meningitis and spent the next month being looked after by the nurses at Mounsal Hospital, Manchester.

So for me the 1963 season ended over a month early and I missed out on a score or more end-of-season meetings.

Despite the meningitis I was still happy to finish off the season as I did – having won the major championship in my last meeting.

A far cry from my Wimbledon days . . . and evidence to myself that I could make a career out of British speedway.

7

The Black Sheep . . .

Even when I was a starry-eyed teenager seeking speedway fame I had one major ambition.

To do well in the World Championship. And it was this burning ambition that brought me one of the hardest decisions I have ever had to make in speedway.

It was simply – should I stand by a man who had given me my second chance in British speedway and give up my World Championship hopes for at least one season. Or should I turn my back on the World Championship and risk possible suspension as a blackleg.

The choice was left to me and the reason for the choice was that the administrators of speedway's two leagues in the early sixties, the senior National League and the junior but highly successful Provincial League had fallen out.

The Auto-Cycle Union had decided that the National League was the party acting within its jurisdiction and warned the riders that if they chose to ride in the Provincial League they would be competing on unlicensed tracks and once they had done that they would not be eligible to compete in the World Championship.

I had, the previous season, ridden for Provincial League Newcastle although it was still claimed that technically I was on Wimbledon's books as my name had been on their retained list from 1958 until the year I came back to Britain.

After my bout of meningitis at the back end of 1963 I began to plan and look forward to 1964. Even in those days my prime object was to do well in the World Championship and you can imagine the blow when I heard I might be robbed of an opportunity to compete.

Mike Parker and his fellow Provincial League promoters withdrew from the Control Board and the F.I.M., and as I had been the top rider in the Provincial League in 1963 I was sure I could ride for practically any team in the National League. And a National League place would have been a passport to the World Championship rounds.

Instead I agreed to stay with Newcastle although all along I believed that the internal disputes would be settled in time for the World Championship rounds.

I think that I rode well enough that season to have reached the World Final but I never had the chance to see if my confidence was justified or not.

Even though I had a really good season and won just about every individual meeting there was – including a second Provincial League Riders Championship and a long spell as holder of the individual Silver Sash – I wasn't happy when the year was over.

To me it was nothing more than a year of frustration and a wasted year. Till then I had spent far too many wasted years and it was only the fact that Mike Parker had brought me over when National League promoters hadn't even answered my letters that I stayed in the Provincial League.

I was even more determined than ever not to waste any more time and had the split between the two leagues not been solved during the winter I would definitely have joined a National League track in 1965 if that was to be the only way I was to ride in the World Championship.

Fortunately, though, the winter brought its rewards and both leagues amalgamated to form one big league in 1965 and once again I was ready to help Newcastle – and try and get somewhere in the World Championship.

The way might have been clear as far as a licence was concerned but other circumstances played a big part in my 1965 season.

For I spent practically all that season injured.

I had an opening meeting at Wolverhampton on the Good Friday and had a collision with Australian Gordon Guasco who later lost his life in a track crash in Australia.

It was my second race and my left leg ended up in Gordon's engine as we turned into the corner. I smashed my left ankle very badly and was rushed to hospital for surgery.

I was in hospital for some time and had to have a couple of screws put into the ankle to hold it together. I eventually discharged myself from the Manchester Hospital because they wanted me to stay in hospital for another month or six weeks and all the time I was in there the speedway season was passing me by without a second thought.

Whenever I talked to the specialist about riding speedway again in six or seven weeks he shrugged his shoulders. I think they looked on me as something of an idiot.

After I had discharged myself I contacted Dr Carlo Biagi who was then at a hospital at Galashiels in Scotland. Dr Biagi had been the track doctor at Southampton and had become quite a dedicated speedway fan.

Besides his intense personal interest he had also proved to be speedway's number one medical friend and scores of riders had been to him for treatment.

He had a passionate understanding of the inner thoughts of the speedway rider and did everything in his power to assist in their recovery. It was this reputation that made me realise that if I was to carry on riding during the 1965 season it was Dr Biagi who would make it possible.

I went up to Scotland and he continued to treat me and on every trip he would take the plaster off, re-set my foot a little bit and put plaster back on it until eventually we were getting the plaster down a bit and getting my foot in an upward position. We were striving to get the foot into such a position that we could get a steel shoe to fit right round the plaster so that I could ride in my first World Championship qualifying rounds which was set down for Newcastle on Monday, 14th June.

I had a practice the week before but it was impossible for me to ride then although I realised that when the championship came round I could put an extra effort into it and sure enough that is what happened.

In the pits I needed crutches to hop around but once on the bike I forgot any pain I had and at the end of the evening I was happy to have got second place with eleven points.

Trying to ease the pain under the shower in the changing room I wondered whether the foot would stand up to another two tough qualifying rounds at Glasgow and Edinburgh.

At least I had three clear days before my next meeting but I didn't relish the thought of having to risk the foot at Glasgow on the Friday and Edinburgh the following night.

During those four days we changed the plaster and continued working on the foot to try and give it extra movement and I had my second round at Glasgow. Again I needed the crutches in the pits but qualified for the semi-finals with a total of 23 points from my two Scottish meetings.

I'm convinced that if I had stayed at the Manchester Hospital I wouldn't have been able to compete in any of the early rounds and it was only the amazing medical ability of Dr Biagi that allowed me to take to the track at all.

Between the Edinburgh meeting and my semi-final at Glasgow I had nearly a month during which time I kept up my regular trips to see Dr Biagi for a change of plaster and manipulation. It was quite plain that my leg was getting stronger as each week passed.

We made another steel shoe to cover the leg which was still in plaster and I finished fourth in the Glasgow semi-final and clinched a place in the British Final due to be staged at West Ham a month later.

As I had never gone so far in the championship in previous years I really began praying that everything would go well and I would be able to ride at my peak.

By now I was riding again regularly and the plaster was due to come off before the West Ham meeting. Strength came flowing back into the damaged ankle and as it did so my scores started to improve again and I began to feel physically capable of the task ahead of me.

On the Friday before the British Final I was riding at Newport but finished up in hospital again – smashing my right hand on a safety fence at Somerton Park.

Foolishly I agreed to ride for my club Newcastle the next night at Wimbledon and partly because I was unable to hold on to the handlebar properly and partly because my partner Brian Brett and I touched handlebars while at the end of the straight I got into a bit of trouble and went off over the top of the bike, breaking eight bones in the right foot.

So here I was with my left ankle just out of the plaster and faced with a British Final with an injured hand and eight broken bones in my right foot!

Three days in which to build up enough strength to try to get through!

Then, dramatically in a season when nothing seemed to go right the heavens opened and the rain poured down . . . and I was happy. For it rained so hard that the British Final had to be called off and I had another seven days in which to try and recover.

Newcastle had a match at Halifax on the Saturday before the re-run of the British Final and I wanted to ride in this.

And that was probably what cost me a place in the World Final! Certainly it will always rate as one of the biggest mistakes I have made in my career because all it did was to aggravate the injury to my right hand and to my leg.

I'd had so many pain-killing injections and drugs over the past month or two that when I got to the West Ham meeting the doctor refused to give me any more injections.

I'll never forget that when the other fifteen riders went out for the parade prior to the start of the meeting I went into the ambulance room and sat there and gave myself injections between my toes, in the heel, in between my fingers and in the palm of my hand!

I scored about five points that night when nine would have been enough to qualify so I missed out by about four points in the end. As far as I was concerned the season might just as well have ended there and the only thing left to do was ride out the rest of the season as best I could.

Certainly I was looking forward to going back home to New Zealand, training and getting fit again for the start of 1966.

Before the season was over, however, I tried to win the British League Riders Championship final at Belle Vue, but again the old injury bogey raised its ugly head.

After winning my first outing I fell in my second race and once again aggravated the old leg injuries and only managed five points from my remaining three rides.

I rode fewer meetings in 1965 than in any other season in British speedway and also dropped far more points than I had done the year before.

For most of the year I had to wear the special boot and was forced to adopt something of a different style although I never really thought about it at the time.

It was with some relief that I finished the season in one piece and I was glad to get home to New Zealand for what was planned as a holiday from speedway.

As I flew into Christchurch the last thing on my mind was riding speedway again and I felt that what I needed was a long break to build up to 100 per cent fitness again. And I could think of no better place in which to do that than New Zealand.

However it didn't work like that, because I was talked into riding at Christchurch. It wasn't as bad as it sounded though, because it meant riding only once a week – Saturday night – and the rest of the week I spent running up and down sandhills near my home.

These were the hills I used to train in when I was a kid involved in athletics and I believed that it was the easiest way to recover my full fitness. But the more I trained the more pain I got from the two screws that had been inserted in my broken ankle. I thought it was just because I was training too much and straining the ankle but eventually the pain became so bad that I had to go to a specialist in Christchurch who x-rayed it and decided that the screws had to come out.

What had happened was that I had been training so hard and bending the ankle at such a great angle running up the hills that the hole where the screws were had simply become sloppy and the screws weren't doing any job at all but just rubbing away at the bone.

Having the screws out was just like going to the dentists to have a tooth out. The expectation was worse than reality. Once the screws had been pulled out the ankle felt much better and I was in nowhere near as much pain as I had been.

I had to wait 14 or 15 days before I could start training again but once they had taken the stitches out I was able to do a bit of light training and gradually increased it until I was running two or three miles a day.

So when I got back to England at Easter in 1966 I was feeling fitter than I had been for some time and was ready to tackle the new season with the worries and disappointments of the 1965 season behind me.

Injuries had completely destroyed my 1965 season. They had not only ended my World Championship hopes but they had also robbed me of the Silver Sash Match Race Championship – Peter Jarman took it from me by default in the second half of the opening meeting at Wolverhampton when I broke my ankle and I never had a chance to challenge for it again all season. It also denied me any chance of challenging Barry Briggs for the Golden Helmet Match Race Championship and also put me out of the running for the Great Britain team that had five test matches against the Soviet Union, and for the five man British side that went over to Kempten, West Germany, for the World Team Cup.

I don't think it is any false modesty if I say that had I been fit I could have got into the test teams and the World Cup party. In fact during 1965 only one title had come my way – the relatively unimportant Northern Star Trophy which I won with a maximum at Newcastle.

So I knew no matter what happened it would need to be a catastrophic season if I wasn't to improve in 1966 on my 1965 record.

Things were a lot better. Within a meeting or two of the season started I knew that I would feel no real ill effects from my earlier injuries and began to look forward to the World Championship with eager anticipation.

In 1964 I hadn't ridden in the Championship. In 1965 injuries wrecked my hopes. At last I was in a position to do myself justice – and prove that I was capable of holding my own in World class opposition.

I knew I had many critics who still considered that I was capable of beating the ex-Provincial League riders but when it came to matching my skills against those reared on the cut-and-thrust of the old National League I would be outclassed.

I was determined – more determined than I had ever been before – to show them that I was capable of going a long way in the World Championship and it was with this steely determination and a conviction at the back of my mind that I sailed into the 1966 World Championship campaign.

First round was, as luck had it, a home draw at Newcastle. I started out on the right foot and got 15 points there. The next evening I was at Long Eaton and after having engine failure in my first race I won my other four rides so I'd got through the first two meetings unbeaten by an opponent.

My last qualifying round that year was at Hackney and I got eleven points which made sure that I was in the line-up for the semi-final at Halifax.

There I was struggling a little bit but still qualified among the top eight which meant I was in the British Final at Wimbledon. While I wasn't on top form at Halifax I did do what I set out to do – qualify for the next round.

That has been my philosophy throughout the World Championship. I go to a meeting with one major aim – to get those points. If on the way I am going well and realise I have a chance of winning the meeting then I set my sights on that, but initially winning the meeting is of no interest.

I would rather qualify from every meeting than win six European titles and miss out of the seventh occasion. This is what made Ove Fundin and Barry Briggs such great riders.

They had the ability to score enough points even on a bad night to get into the World Final and to some extent this is where so many English riders fall down. They seem more eager to win the meeting outright rather than consider the question of how many points are needed to make progress.

Back though to the British Final at Wimbledon where I got 11 points and finished second.

From Wimbledon the top eight qualifiers went forward to the British/Nordic Final at Sheffield to be joined by the top eight Scandinavians. Again I finshed second to Barry Briggs and joined him in the European Final at Wembley for what was my first ever riding visit to the Empire Stadium.

It was also the first time I had ever been beyond a British Final and I set out with the intention of scoring enough points to get through to Gothenburg. When I finished second to Barry in my first race I took it that once again Barry was going to prove my better.

But he dropped a couple of points and after winning my remaining four rides I found myself with the title European Champion. It was my first major championship title and gave me more satisfaction than anything else up to that time in my career.

Having finished second to Barry in the British Final and the Nordic British Final I was happy to have beaten him for the first time in a big meeting.

To be European champion felt great but most of all I had won a meeting at Wembley which to me was always the place for the World Final. Whenever I have dreamt of winning the World Final it has always been at Wembley and to me this was the crowning moment of my career.

This was one ambition and quite apart from this I had qualified for my first ever World Final.

I've dealt with my first World Final in some detail in a later chapter so here it would suffice to say that after considerable arguments with Newcastle promoter Mike Parker I missed practice at Gothenburg and eventually finished fourth.

While it was a satisfying performance much of the gloss had been rubbed off by the circumstance leading up to the final and I was far from happy with that initial appearance in the World Final.

It could not, though, hide my pleasure at having made my first World Final and if I began to think too much about what had gone on before I only had to turn up the old speedway magazines to read about my 1965 season.

At least I was on the road up and I was able to use the European Title to bring considerable financial advantages particularly on the continent.

After having made the final I often wondered what would have happened had I not spent five years away from British speedway between 1958 and 1963. I still find it terribly difficult to answer.

While I think it may have hastened my final appearance I still believe the experience I gained in Australia had as much to do with a final placing as my English experience.

I did very little during the winter of '66 and '67, deciding to stay in Manchester with my family. I spent more of the time preparing for the 1967 season although I did take six weeks away during the early part of 1967 to compete in the World Ice-Racing Championship in Russia with my Newcastle team-mate Goog Allan.

Throughout the 1966 season I had switched from the Jap machine to the Jawa machine, from track to track and during the winter I spent a great deal of time preparing both types of machine with the help of Guy Allott who, by then, looked after my engines full time.

I wasn't really sure which bike I wanted to ride exclusively because I would ride the Japs on the tracks that I classed as speedway tracks, as against the tracks I classed a halfscramble tracks.

At this time a lot of the tracks were becoming very rough so I started to ride the Jawa more and more, although I rode the Jap more scientifically than the Jawa in those days.

I did a lot more thinking with the Jap and used a lot more throttle control with it not only from the starting line to the first corner, but also throughout the rest of the race.

With the Jawa, when I first started riding it, I really used to just aim it and then fire it full throttle! I definitely did a lot more thinking on the Jap and for that reason rode it in all my World Championship qualifying rounds, semi-finals, finals and so on.

In '67 I started out on the Jawa and got a 15-point maximum at Hackney Wick in my opening meeting and that was a lucky omen, for once again I got through to the World Final – this time at Wembley which at least presented no problems as far as getting there for practice was concerned.

I had ridden the Jawa in quite a number of meetings, leading up to the final but once again I abandoned it in favour of the Jap. I preferred using the Jap for gating and because I felt it would be better around the tight corners of Wembley. I had, in fact, taken both machines to the practice and had a couple of laps on the Jawa before making the decision to go British so to speak.

I spent the weeks leading up to the final, planning everything in minute details and must have spent hundreds of hours in the workshop checking, re-checking and generally trying to ensure that nothing would go wrong with the bike on September 16th.

I was quite confident that I would be able to repeat my European Final success and nothing that happened in my first three races made me think otherwise.

Briggo was the pre-meeting favourite with his main opposition expected to come from Russian Igor Plechanov, Swede Bengt Jansson and possibly one of the Poles.

A few days before the final I had almost missed Newcastle's league match against Edinburgh because of a plane delay coming back from the Continent but I knew that I was in fine fettle when I took a 15-point maximum from Sheffield two days before the final.

I knew that the bike was going and I knew that physically and mentally I was attuned to the task of trying for my first World title.

As I have written, I won my first three rides, beating possible challengers Plechanov in heat four; Anton Woryna in heat eight and Briggo in heat nine.

I was beginning to feel that I was going to repeat that Wembley triumph of twelve months previous. In the pits I tried to adjust my thoughts and mentally I was prepared for the big clash – with Ove Fundin who was unbeaten after three rides and Bengt Jansson who had dropped only a single point.

The programme showed I was to meet Jansson in heat 15 and Fundin three races later. It also showed I was off the inside against Jansson and even though I made the gate the fiery Swede cut through on the inside on the third bend of the second lap. Nothing I could do could get back the lead but I was still in with a chance with 11 out of 12 points.

Fundin, two races earlier, lost his unbeaten tally when he was beaten by the flying Russian Plechanov, so after four rides I was level on 11 points with Fundin, Jansson and Plechanov.

The path to the Triple Crown. *Left:* British Champion, Wimbledon, 1968. *Below:* European Champion for the first time at Wembley, 1966, with runner-up Barry Briggs (right) and Anton Woryna

World Champion at last – and the traditional way of celebrating at Gothenburg, 1968

A year later, and it's Championship No. 2 at Wembley

And finally, the Triple Crown flanked by the Polish pai Waloszek (left) and Woryn who were second and thir 1970

I had beaten Plechanov. Plechanov had beaten Fundin. Jansson had beaten me. And Fundin had beaten Jansson.

In my fifth race I was up against Ove Fundin, his fellow countrymen Bernie Persson and Pole Andy Pogorzelski. If either Fundin or I won the race we could win the title – or at the worst finish second.

I'll never forget that race. Fundin was off number one position on the inside and I was off number four on the outside. We both gated about the same and we both went into the turn approximately the same. I was on the outside and then my world was really shattered.

Suddenly Bernie Persson who came from position three, somehow rode straight into me as we were about a quarter or a third of the way into the corner and the bike and I went flying all over the place.

That in a nutshell was the end of the World Championship in 1967. 'Persson was disqualified immediately by the referee but that didn't help me very much because I was lying in a big heap with a bruised leg, bent handlebars, bent forks and a slightly twisted back frame. I had to prepare immediately to ride against Fundin.

Besides having to go into my last race with a slightly bent frame I must admit that my confidence was dented. I had felt on top of the world after winning my first three rides and honestly thought I was only eight laps away from the world title.

It is, I am sure, something that wouldn't affect me today but it did at Wembley and I finished third with 13 points while Fundin and Jansson had a run-off after tieing on fourteen points, with Fundin winning.

I must say that the heat 18 was one of the most disturbing situations I have even been involved in. After Persson had been disqualified he argued fiercely with the referee Mr Arthur Humphrey and it wasn't until he was threatened with suspension from further World Championship meetings that he agreed to leave the track.

All this time I was busy trying to straighten my bike, and the extra experience of Ove Fundin showed in the end and he beat me in the re-run of that race as he led me out of the gate.

Third position was an improvement of one position on the previous year and at least I was on the rostrum. I still felt I was making progress but as far as the World Championship was concerned I would only be completely satisfied with first place.

8

The World Crown, It's All Mine

Nothing meant anything in 1968. Nothing except . . . the World Championship.

I knew that my days with Newcastle were numbered and throughout a stormy season I kept riding for one reason only – so that I could have another go at that elusive World Champions title.

Inwardly I knew I was capable of winning it. The harsh realities of the 1967 Wembley final bit deep into my mind and probably left a bitterness that was to prove to be vital in my climb.

For me the 1968 season started in February – with a phone call that was to have a lasting effect on my career.

Throughout 1967 I had made repeated visits to the Continent and as the season progressed so the rumours mounted – that the Czechoslovakian machine manufacturers Jawa were willing to sponsor me with a work's contract.

I hadn't been officially approached by anyone connected with the company and at this time I still preferred to ride the Jap machine although I had been using the Jawa on some of the rougher English tracks.

It was with this in mind that I sat down one day in February to make a phone call to the Jap agents in London with a simple request: Would they provide me with Jap machines to ride.

The response was probably what I had expected – they were not interested. At that time Jap still had a virtual monopoly in this country and only a handful of riders were mounted on the foreign machines.

Once I had been told there was nothing doing I decided to make an all out effort to see if there really was anything in the previous season's rumours.

I decided to ride the Jawa as often as I could and even though the Jap was perfectly prepared it sat in my workshop for most of the first few months of the 1968 season.

So determined was I to get a works contract with Jawa – a contract that would eventually be worth thousands of pounds per season – that I forgot about my leaning towards the British engine and risked using the Jawa in every single World Championship event in which I rode during 1968.

When the World Championship draw was announced I found my first meeting was at Belle Vue on 25th May. A quick look at my diary confirmed my fears – I had already contracted to compete in a meeting in Germany on the same day.

I asked the Speedway Control Board if they would change my first round but they refused to do it . . . and I had to miss my European jaunt.

Rain tumbled down as only it can tumble down in Manchester, and it was a sodden, wet, miserable night when I wheeled the Jawa out for one of the rare occasions on which I had used it in the World Championship up till that time.

Gating was of paramount importance in the rain – it is always far harder to pass an opponent on a wet track because of the thick spray and shale thrown up by the rear wheels which can often leave you momentarily blind – and the Jawa behaved perfectly.

As silky as a running cat and as powerful as a roaring lion the trusty Jawa picked up the grip out of the gate and I found myself going into the first turn ahead of my opponents in all five starts. From there it was a relatively easy job keeping in front particularly under the conditions.

Fifteen points in the bag from Manchester . . . and on to my home track at Newcastle for what looked on paper one of the easiest rounds of the championship.

On the day of the meeting Pete Jarman, Allan Butterfield and Alf Wells dropped out through various reasons and juniors had to take their place in the meeting.

Chief opposition was, as I had expected, Barry Briggs and we clashed in heat eighteen when we were both unbeaten with 12 points. Again the Jawa was gating and I held off Briggo's challenge for the four laps to keep my unbeaten record.

At this time I had been riding the Jawa all season and gaining in confidence as each league meeting passed. At the beginning of June I was still unbeaten by an opponent in league racing and never have

I gone into the World Championship so confident of getting through.

But at the back of my mind was always the one fear that I would have a disastrous meeting in which I wouldn't score. The always-impending threat of an engine seizure weighed heavily on my mind and that is why I always took at least two machines to every World Championship meeting.

It is an old, but nonetheless true saying, that no meeting is won until the last race. And in the World Championship you can add – until the last round!

Going to West Ham for my final qualifying rounds I knew that no matter how many points I scored I would almost certainly get through into the semi-final.

Maybe this unconsciously had an effect or maybe I was beaten by better riders on the night. Whatever it was I dropped two points – one to maximum man Norman Hunter and the other to Nigel Boocock – but it was still more than enough to ensure a semi-final place at Poole in the last couple of days of June.

While the Jawa was performing near perfectly in the league and World Championship rounds I was going through one of those infuriating spells in international meetings.

I just hit one snag after another and ran together a string of the lowest scores I have ever had in internationals since making my debut. Everything, though, seemed to be sorted out in time for the semi-final at Poole.

Up early, as usual, and the long drive down to the South Coast with rain practically all the way, ended as so many major championship meetings seem to end . . . with no racing.

The waterlogged track was in such a dreadful state that the referee had no option but to declare the meeting off – and re-arrange it for the following Tuesday.

I was more than a little worried lest anything should go wrong mechanically for I was riding at Newcastle 24 hours before the Poole semi-final. I worked it out that I would just about have time for a couple of hours sleep at home before leaving for Poole.

All plans, though, would be scattered far and wide if I ran into trouble during Newcastle's league match with Newport.

Again the wipers to'd and fro'd across the windscreen as the rain swept down on the drive up to Tyneside. As a precaution I had loaded the Jap on to the trailer and intended using it all night in case I ruined the Jawa.

It was still raining when I arrived in Newcastle but the clouds broke up and the meeting started on time on a wet but rideable track. Then after only two heats a thunderclap shattered the inter-heat silence and the heavens opened.

There was no more racing and I was on my way back to Manchester for an unexpected few extra hours sleep before the journey down to Poole. It was obvious from the second heat that Martin Ashby was the man to beat as he took a slice out of the track record.

Come the last heat of the meeting and we lined up alongside each other. I was unbeaten but Martin had dropped a solitary point in an earlier heat to Reg Luckhurst.

All four in the heat had enough points to give them a place in the British Final – so it was between Martin and myself for the £30 winner's cheque. It was Martin's turn to take the honours so it meant we had to meet again in the run-off to decide who would take the £30 – and the top place. This time I had my revenge so drove home – again in the rain – a happy man.

Besides pocketing an extra £30 I had qualified for the British Final. I had only one regret – it was on my bogey track Wimbledon.

Close season work during the winter had seen the Wimbledon management completely re-shape and tighten the Plough Lane circuit. On a previous visit this season – for the big Internationale and its prize of a new speedway machine – I had struggled from the word go and finished way down near the foot of the scorers with only four points.

A second chance to adjust to the new shape had been denied me when I cried off the Great Britain v. Sweden test match because of German measles. So on the night I was very much less fancied than Barry Briggs, the man who had won the previous five British Finals!

But it was a position I was accustomed to – in Briggo's shadow. And a position I was determined to reverse by the end of 1968.

Despite my rows with Newcastle – by now made public – I had maintained my league form and had become so well suited to riding the Jawa that I had hardly noticed the switch-over.

Before the British Final, though, speedway was to suffer a blow when popular Eddie Glennon – the man who had met me on the Southampton quayside – died in a car accident while returning in the early hours from running a meeting at Newport.

His death was yet another reminder of the hazards that have to be faced off the track. Even though Eddie was very much involved in my bickering with the Newcastle management his death came as a blow, as I considered him a friend. He had always gone out of his way to help me and my family and made my early days in Manchester a bearable passage. His death hit speedway as badly as it hit me, and it was fitting that many of the country's top riders, volunteered to ride in a special memorial meeting to his memory.

The British Final brought me a 15-point maximum and deprived Briggo of his title. Eric Boocock, Trevor Hedge, Martin Ashby, Nigel Boocock, Norman Hunter, Jim McMillan, Terry Betts and Dave Younghusband edged through to join me in the penultimate step to the final – a British Nordic Final at one of my all-time favourite circuits . . . West Ham.

The British Final had proved what a brave collection of riders are involved in top class speedway. The sick-list roll-call before the meeting would have done credit to any 'Emergency Ward Ten' film script!

Barry Briggs had a broken thumb in plaster. Nigel Boocock had a broken collar-bone strapped up. Ray Wilson had his left ankle smothered in plaster. And Trevor Hedge climbed out of a sick bed where he had been suffering from flu.

Maybe they all seem relatively minor injuries but I can assure you that the slightest physical handicap does little to improve ones chances of success in speedway! Perhaps it is significant that all four invalids dredged up hidden reserves of strength to outscore their fitter rivals. . . .

It had been fourteen years since Barry Briggs had made his World Final debut. And West Ham was to mark his exit from the championship arena – or so it seemed.

Briggo hadn't ridden since the British Final and his broken thumb was still far from right.

No matter how hard he tried he couldn't recapture the form of which we all knew he was capable and it was a sad and sorry Barry who trundled out of the pits as a non qualifier with but half a dozen points. As it turned out he was to get another chance through a chain of circumstances and he was to ride in the Final. But to all intents and purposes it seemed his final sequence was broken.

Unhappily too, a great number of fans, and one or two riders, seemed to take great glee in Briggo's apparent downfall. Little did they realise the courage of the man.

While Briggo suffered I rejoiced – and added the British/Nordic title to my British title and headed the eight-strong party booked for the European final.

How close I came to missing out on the trip I will never know. But things might have worked out differently. Besides the Jawa I rode in all five races I brought along a spare machine so that I could switch to it if trouble set in at any time.

I warmed the bike up and it stood ready to be used if the need arose. My Newcastle team-mate Ole Olsen was also using the machine and when he broke a footrest he took the spare bike on to the track needing a heat win to get through to his first final.

He never even made the first bend – for he was excluded under the two minute rule. There had been no fuel in the spare machine! I had in fact been close to using it myself because a float broke in the carburettor and but for having a few heats gap between races I would have automatically ridden the spare machine if my races had been closer together.

To this day I have tried to make 100 per cent certain that my spare machine has always been topped up – and I'll never know how it came to be empty at West Ham. Ole, obviously, was extremely upset about it . . . but he was to reach a final two seasons later.

I began to realise how a footballer feels during the interminable wait between the semi-final and the F.A. Cup Final. Everything built up to a climax. Practically every race was overshadowed by the fear of injury that might have kept me out of the Wroclaw meeting.

I knew that the European Final was *THE* vital meeting. All the season's work; all the season's worry; and all the season's effort would count for nothing if I failed to make it in Wroclaw.

Had it still been the middle-sixties I would have had little confidence on the bumpy flight out of London. No one really expected the British contingent to challenge the team riding East Europeans when it came to fighting out a European Final behind the Iron Curtain.

However, I had confidence in myself. I doubted that I could win the European title – but I was equally convinced that I was capable of scoring enough points to book my place for a second Gothenburg World Final.

A few days before the party boarded the charter flight Norman

Hunter went down with flu so Briggo, by now slowly recovering from his injury, came along on the trip as reserve.

Eventually he was to ride as unlucky Eric Boocock had to pull out of the final with a virus. The fact that a Polish doctor was willing to certify him too ill to ride proved how poorly Eric was for I'm sure the Poles would have felt more confident had Briggo not been among the riders who went on the traditional pre-meeting presentation march.

Shrouded in political drapes the meeting proved only one thing – that the Poles weren't quite as good as they would have us believe. While they filled the top three places (and four of the ten qualifying spots) I had the satisfaction of beating both European champion Pawel Waloszek and second place man Anton Woryna.

Having broken the Wroclaw track record I had showed myself that there was nothing to fear in the Poles that there wasn't to fear in every other World class rider.

Throughout the trip to Poland the news was of the Russian invasion of Czechoslovakia and a few hours before the final the Norwegian Motor Federation ordered their two riders, Sverre Harrfeldt and Reidar Eide not to compete in the meeting because of the political implications.

Each and every one of the British contingent was given the option to drop out of the final – but eventually everyone agreed to ride. And Harrfeldt and Eide disobeyed their orders.

Tragically Harrfeldt's decision was to take an unwarranted slice out of his career when he clipped Eddie Janacarz's rear wheel in his third race and had to be rushed to the University of Wroclaw Hospital with serious injuries to his pelvis, thigh-bone and ankle.

Although we were all able to visit Sverre before leaving Poland it was no consolation that of a British party of six, four had qualified for the final . . . including Briggo who scored two heat wins in his ten points.

Sverre was to stay in Poland bed-ridden for another month and even to this day he still wears the savage scars of that heat 12 crash. Bravely though the Norwegian had survived a series of crippling blows, he has spent two years trying to recover his pre-accident form.

Having headed the non-Polish qualifiers with eleven points I felt confident as I prepared for the final in Gothenburg.

The now familiar, but nonetheless depressing, confrontation with

Mike Parker again resulted in my request to miss Newcastle's Monday evening meeting being turned down.

This time, though, I wasn't at the disadvantage I had been in 1966. I had seen the Gothenburg track; I had ridden the track; and I had made a note of the correct gear ratio in the little brown book of facts and figures I always carry around with me.

I had a few meetings between Wroclaw and Gothenburg – but it gave me enough time to spend practically every minute inspecting the two bikes I was to take with me.

I had learned that more important than anything was to finish five races in the World final and on the Monday before the final I tried out a brand new Jawa at Newcastle.

Nothing in the world could have sounded sweeter than that engine as it powered me to a comfortable maximum. But more important I was gating well.

In fact I think I was gating better than at any time in my career – before or since – and I was full of confidence as I touched down at the Gothenburg Airport.

Confidence is something that is an essential ingredient of a champion's make-up. But it has to be the right degree. Too much is dangerous. And too little equally so.

Mentally I was prepared for the big push. Before each final my routine is the same . . . concentrate on nothing but. During a meeting I will scarcely talk even to my mechanics. There is no need. They know what to do and I know they will do it.

High up in the stands I knew that Raye was mentally – and perhaps physically – crossing her fingers. At home the three children were waiting for Late Night Extra . . . and the promised World Final report which was due round about ten p.m. that Friday night.

All this was at the back of my mind. But it rarely had a chance to filter through as the long hours of pre-final preparation began. Check the chain. The fuel. The tyres. The gear ratio. The throttle cable. The clutch plates. The handlebars. The seat. The forks, front and back. Look at the track. Watch. Think. And above all concentrate.

A quick look at the programme and I realised that my first heat opponents included Barry Briggs. That was good. Briggo is a notorious slow starter and I'd much rather meet him in the first race than later on. Notorious slow starter? By his standards – but not by anyone else's.

I knew if I could beat Briggo in the first one I must be in with a chance. If I had suffered during 1965 it was Briggo's turn in 1968. After his British Final broken thumb he was shivering in the pits showing the effects of a mysterious virus. But I knew that wouldn't stop him once he was out on track.

As I had hoped – as I had planned – I made the gate. Possibly one of the finest gates in my life. And it took me ahead of Briggo and Poland's bright hope Janacarz. I held it for four laps and as the flag signalled the end of the race I had beaten the man I always considered my chief opponent.

But in a World final no one is incapable of winning. That's why they are there. Race by race passed; and race by race I gated and won. Until there were no races left and I had won my first World Championship title.

I was in a daze and even today I can't honestly say how I felt as I received the World Championship trophy from 20-year-old Mona Samuelsson, Sweden's Miss Speedway.

My wife Raye came out of her seat next to her friend Pam Oakes and down on the track to greet me on my lap of honour. At home I'm sure the kids were jumping for joy as the late Peter Arnold's voice came over loud and clear from Gothenburg with the message that the 1970 World Speedway Champion was New Zealander Ivan Mauger.

My mechanics Bob Hall and Tony Shelley – who changed my rear tyre in between each race – were as excited as I, and we all spent forty minutes or so trying to grasp exactly what it all meant.

The traditional winner's banquet started – without the winner as Raye and I collected our thoughts and realised that a life's ambition had come through in the calm of the Swedish air.

Everything that had gone before was pushed way back in our minds. The struggles. The arguments. The heart-aches. And the triumphs. All somehow pale into insignificant insignificance compared to the thrill of a first World title. . . .

9

Two in a Row

Having won the World title once what was there left, you may ask?

The answer simply . . . another World Final.

Maybe, I had thought, in the days following my Gothenburg win, the will to continue riding would fade as the winter months passed.

My winter threat to stay at home unless I moved from a Mike Parker track was no idle stick waved in the heat of the moment. I was determined to have my move . . . even if it meant retiring from the sport with a world title as the main reward.

I knew that the title was a passport to continental riches and while it would not have been without tears I was prepared to quit speedway altogether.

As it happened, I didn't need to carry out the threat and eventually I had my wish . . . joining Belle Vue for the 1969 season.

The Gothenburg victory had done nothing to dim my enthusiasm. I wanted not only to add a second World title to my name – but I wanted to lead Belle Vue to further honours.

I had always considered that Wembley was the rightful home of the World Championship and it was with the thought of climbing the rostrum at the Wembley stadium that I set out on the 1969 pathway.

The rumours of 12 months previous – that I would be offered a works contract with the Jawa concern – came to fruition as they approached me in a few days after the World final, and a few days before my 29th birthday on 12th October to ask if I would ride for them.

I had no hesitation and that was the first major contract that I signed as World Champion. How many people realise, though, that had I been offered support from Britain's Jap agents I would have accepted, as at that time I still considered the Jap a better machine for my needs.

I had, though, become accustomed to the Jawa and there's little doubt that I prefer it today.

A round-the-world racing trip meant I missed Belle Vue's two opening matches of the season against Sheffield but I arrived back in Manchester in time for a special Good Friday clash with Halifax . . . determined to lift the Aces up the league table.

And certainly the way we started off the 1969 season it seemed that league honours would come thundering back to Hyde Road. By the time the draw for the qualifying rounds of the championship were announced the Aces led the British League table – and neither Soren Sjosten nor myself had dropped a point to an opponent.

Qualifying rounds took me to Poole, Wimbledon and my home track Belle Vue where I had a maximum that added up to 41 points and a certain place in the British semi-finals. Particularly pleasing because at one time I had feared that I wouldn't be able to take part in the rounds!

I'd been riding in Germany the Sunday before my first round at Poole when I'd come off at something like 90 mile an hour. I spent the next few days with my shoulder strapped up and my head aching – too scared to go to see my doctor just in case he ordered me to take a rest. The Aces were still top of the league and after eleven matches in which I'd not dropped a single league point I went to Kings Lynn and lost to both Malcolm Simmons and Clive Featherby.

Also my chances of winning the televised Internationale came down to earth when I fell in a run-off with home rider Trevor Hedge – a matter that I have dealt with in a later chapter.

Forget about the league and the big meetings though, for I was still relentlessly pursuing the World Championship goal and with Guy Allott's expert help I was, even then, busy preparing an engine which I hoped I would need for the Wembley Final.

One interesting sidelight to the season came in June when I chalked up my 69th win . . . and became the proud winner of a case of Vat 69 whisky. I didn't have too much time to drink it though, as I needed to be in top physical shape for the Sheffield semi-final on Thursday, 26th June.

A few days earlier my arch-rival Briggo had shown that when it came to the World Championship he was going to be the man to beat with a superlative display in the Leicester semi-final.

The rivalry between us was such that having at last escaped from his shadow I was eager to at least emulate his performance. While I did not score a similar 15-point maximum at least I had the satisfaction of topping the scorers after beating Ray Wilson in a run-off.

A few heats earlier I had been last away from the tapes in my clash with Ray and nothing I could do could take me past him. However Ray was filled in in his last ride and dropped an unexpected point to veteran Scot Ken McKinlay.

Next step in the fight to retain the crown was the British Final at West Ham where I experienced my worst meeting of the entire 1969 tournament.

By now there was quite a bit of sniping going on through various speedway columns and one writer described me as 'one of Nature's scowlers.'

He went on to add: 'Most of you reckon he is scowling. Most of you reckon he is therefore perpetually bad-tempered, aggravated and annoyed. Particularly when he's been beaten.

'I pass on this bit of good public relations advice to Ivan. Force yourself to smile mate.'

At least I had reason to smile. I had strung together a long row of race wins and, in the middle of July, was still unbeaten at Belle Vue in an official meeting.

But it was certainly true to say that I was by no means speedway's number one pin-up boy. Throughout my career my critics had claimed I was moody and stand-offish. Probably because I didn't rush up to them in a bar, throw my arm around their shoulders and buy them a drink.

But that wasn't the way I did things. Certainly I've never deliberately ignored anyone but I must admit that I did find it difficult to strike up conversations with people I didn't know.

None of this caused any worry though as I got down to what I was being paid for . . . winning races. Belle Vue's position at the top of the table was being challenged by South Coast outfit Poole who, while lacking a real world-class star, were proving that seven good men and true can always produce that little extra needed to turn defeat into victory.

With four away victories to their credit and an unbeaten home record the Pirates had a slight edge on us. While we were still unbeaten at Hyde Road our eight away matches had only brought a couple of victories.

The day before the British Final at West Ham I was to have ridden in a qualifying round of the unimportant Northern Riders Championship and I felt that I needed the time that I should have spent driving up to Newcastle working on my bike which had been giving me a little bit of trouble.

I wasn't at all happy with the Jawa on the Monday and sent a telegram to the Newcastle management saying I wouldn't be able to get there – an action which later meant a Control Board fine – and instead I spent all day Monday in my workshop trying to find out what had been causing the trouble.

I thought I had cured it . . . until my first race at West Ham the following evening. Having melted a piston at Belle Vue on the Saturday preceding I wasn't at all happy with how the bike would perform and I had the galling experience of trailing in last in my first race in the defence of my British title.

I set to, with my mechanics, to find out what was wrong and did so with the result that in my last four rides I lost only to champion Barry Briggs. Eleven points wasn't what I had hoped for – but at least I had come through a depressing final with fourth place. And, more important, a guaranteed place for my second Wembley final.

Quite a few of my old rivals also qualified through the West Ham meeting. Probably the biggest rival of all, Barry Briggs, extended his final appearances with a fine West Ham performance, and all England rejoiced when Coventry skipper Nigel Boocock picked up enough points to ensure a Wembley trip.

Experience, rather than youthful ambition, dominated the British qualifiers. Ronnie Moore, a finalist before I had started racing; Ken McKinlay – one of the most polished veterans in the sport; and Howard Cole, a vastly under-rated Welshman who rode for Kings Lynn, joined Briggo, Booey and myself. Of the six, only Cole could be considered as a youthful contender. And even he had been riding since the early sixties. None of the young brash brigade had made it.

Our league chances took a decided turn for the worse when first Norman Nevitt was dropped and then Bill Powell retired.

Poole, enhancing their reputation as likely champions, kept adding up the points away from home and a few weeks before the World Final I knew that the first half of my double target had been lost.

It left only Wembley. And the strain of the weeks immediately before the big night on 13th September. Five weeks is a hell of a long time to wait for anything . . . and it seems more like five months when a world title and £1,000 is on the end of the line.

I had been experimenting in league and open meetings with nitro-methane but was still a little wary of its possible effects. So I used the weeks up to 13th September to learn as much as I could – but not enough to risk it – about the fuel – and studied all the literature I could lay my hands on about the Wembley track.

As there had been no league racing at the Empire Stadium for many years I knew that there would be no home track advantage and as long as I didn't suffer as at West Ham I had a fine chance of keeping the title. To me that meant everything.

As I have said earlier in this chapter, I have always associated the World Final with Wembley. Like fish and chips they are synonymous. To win at Wembley would give me even more pleasure than to win at Gothenburg. Or so I thought.

Incidentally, a few days after the British Final, Mike Parker announced that he was willing to back Newcastle's new star Ole Olsen against the World Champion. And he was apparently willing to put up a £25 sidestake. Certainly this was of no interest as far as I was concerned. Under no account was I willing to ride for him at Newcastle in anything other than an official fixture.

So the challenge remained unanswered.

I will always remember the Wembley final as yet another controversial episode in a career that has hardly been plain sailing all the way along.

Unbeaten in four rides I came to my fifth outing knowing that I had kept the title – even if I fell off. Team-mate Soren Sjosten was also in the heat needing a win to give him a run-off with Briggo for second spot. It was Sjosten who won . . . much to the disgust of a large section of the crowd.

It was obvious to the crowd that I hadn't tried to beat Sjosten.

AND THAT WAS TRUE. Once he had got out of the gate slightly in front of me I was content to follow him around. Why should I do anything else when the championship was already won? But I assure you Sjosten didn't, as has been suggested, pay me to let him win!

Earlier I'd had a lucky escape from possible serious injury when, in heat nine, I was in against Briggo, spectacular Swede Torbjorn Harryson and Poland's outsider Edward Jancarz who had finished third in Sweden the previous year.

Jancarz and I tore round the first bend as near to locked together as any riders can be, and as he broke away from me coming into the back straight he pulled a locker and Harryson, travelling so close, was left with little alternative but to plough straight into the Pole.

Harry, a firm friend who had lived in Manchester during most of his British career, lay prostrate on the red shale track and as soon as I looked back I knew it was a serious injury. He was carted off by the St John Ambulance men and later in the meeting I learned he had broken his leg.

Complications set in and kept Harryson out of speedway for the next eighteen months or so. So with this in the back of my mind, was I going to be foolish enough to try and mix it with Sjosten?

I decided no and ambled along behind him quite happy with the two points that I didn't really need. But at least I was sure of being able to walk to the Royal Box to receive my trophy!

Coventry fans, in particular, strongly resented my last race tactics and made no secret of their feelings as I did a lap of honour. In fact I had robbed their idol Nigel Boocock of a possible third place but this is something I didn't realise until after the race had been completed.

Certainly I was surprised that Nigel hadn't approached me before we all went out for heat twenty to ask me to make sure I beat Sjosten so that he would get a chance of third place. Maybe if he had done so it might have been different!

Wembley, I have always felt, was an easier victory than in Sweden. Not even in my wildest dreams had I imagined I would be afforded the luxury of a last ride that didn't really matter.

Adding to the occasion was the fact that my mother, Rita Mauger, had been holidaying with us in Manchester and had seen her son win the championship.

She was as pleased as a dog with two tails . . . and we celebrated long into the evening.

A week after the final I was off to Poland as part of the British side competing in the World Team Cup – a contest that had given me a winning medal 12 months previous – and although we lost our grip on the cup it provided yet more evidence that there was nothing to fear from Poland.

Four days later I was in Stockholm wearing the New Zealand colours in my first World Best Pairs Final. Partnered by Bobby

On my first visit to Britain Bobby Andrews (*left*) and Ronnie Moore (*right*) helped to keep me out of the Wimbledon side. Years later Bobby was my partner when we won the World's Best Pairs Championship in 1969, a success I repeated in 1970, this time partnering Ronnie!

A fierce battle with rival number one, Barry Briggs, during a Belle Vue *v* Swindon British League match at Manchester's Hyde Road track

Speedway sometimes has its compensations! *Above:* the World Championship Final, 1968, and congratulations from the beautiful Miss Swedish Speedway. *Below:* a kiss from Sabrina

Andrews – Briggo had declined to ride because of a legal battle he was fighting with Swedish newspapers and Ronnie Moore had been injured – I collected an eighteen-point maximum with Bobby following me home on five occasions to bring New Zealand its first major honour of the sixties.

I was almost as proud of that as I had been of retaining the World Championship!

10

And . . . the Triple Crown

No World Final had ever been held behind the Iron Curtain.

No rider had ever won the title three years in a row.

It was with these thoughts that I set out on the path of the Triple Crown.

The arguments of past seasons now being over and disappearing into a backcloth of memories, I was able to capitalise on my two World titles.

Radio and television interviews became part of the working week and I signed a number of lucrative contracts outside riding. What I needed to crown it was another win. But was it possible in Poland?

Ten – or perhaps even five – years sooner I would have doubted my own ability to take on the Poles in their own backyard with little more than a token chance of anything like success. But the European Final and, more recently, the World Team Cup, had bolstered up my confidence.

First, however, was the task of getting there. I don't think I am labouring the point if I say the route to the 1970 final was the hardest that any British-based rider has ever had to face.

Five meetings in Britain would take me only as far as the British/Nordic Final at Coventry which would embrace not only Danish and Norwegian riders but also the top Swedes. Until that final the English and Swedish competitors had been kept apart in the championship.

Get through the British/Nordic Final and there was a long trek to Leningrad to be faced for the European Final. So it was obvious that many lamed soldiers would limp out of the chase well before 6th September – and that winning rounds was of little importance compared to the paramount task of qualifying, step by step. No matter how narrow or close that gap between success and failure was.

It was a philosophy which was well known to me.

Like a good pianist, it is no good playing all the right notes in the quiet of a rehearsal room if you are to stumble over the orchestra in the concert chamber.

My first priority was to make sure that the orchestra didn't cause my downfall *en route* to the Wroclaw concert chamber.

The long, long road to Poland meant an earlier start than usual in the qualifying rounds and they came around before anyone had really had time to settle into the old routine. This, more than anything else, probably caused the early shocks that dominated the April schedule.

I turned in my lowest qualifying round total in three years when I dropped a valve in one race at Belle Vue and then had trouble with my throttle twist-grip in another, in which tough Tyke Arnie Haley pipped me to the line.

I was a far from happy man when I made the long haul down to Exeter for my second qualifier. I know that four points was not a lot to drop but once something goes wrong with a bike you start to think about it and dwell on it for days.

It needs a good run without any troubles at all to bring the confidence back. Also I couldn't afford another bad meeting with a very tight qualifying target.

Exeter brought welcome relief with five wins in a row although something of the glitter was tarnished by an incident involving Belle Vue's Chris Pusey – my team-mate at Hyde Road – and Exeter's Bruce Cribb – my team-mate in the New Zealand test side.

Chris, with a 15-point maximum at Belle Vue two days earlier, was obviously in the sort of mood that nothing was going to stop him and he had a mighty battle with Cribb which ended in the Kiwi breaking his thigh in a collision with the steel safety fence on the heavily banked quarter-mile circuit.

Angry fans threatened the young Liverpudlian with all sorts of things and at one time I thought he was going to walk out of the meeting. But Chris sensibly quietened down and went on to reach his first ever British Final – a wonderful performance for a youngster with so much promise.

By now it was accepted that the two semi-finals would be at Leicester and Sheffield. For a change I drew the Leicester venue. And with it a passage into the British Final at West Ham.

The chance to snatch the British championship back from Barry

Briggs. But in the back of the mind those painful memories of the 1969 Final.

Would the gremlins strike again? Yet again I made a poor start in my opening heat but this time I was on song and got through to a second place proving that I not only had the right gear for the Custom House track but that the bike was pulling well and performing beautifully.

After that I picked up another four wins although in two of them I had to come from the back to take up the running. The British Championship for the second time. But unlike the other occasions there was still a long way to go before the meeting that really mattered.

To me there was one vital meeting in the busy schedule – the British Nordic Final at Coventry. I considered that would be the hardest task of all. And it was.

Before then I had retained the World Best Pairs Championship for New Zealand – with Ronnie Moore as a partner – and my league form, while not quite as good as the season before, was one of the reasons that Belle Vue were heading the table.

Another was the solid consistency of Soren Sjosten and the remarkable scoring improvement of Pusey who had cast away his inferiority complex and was willing to mix it with the best.

I set myself an eight-point target for the Wednesday evening meeting at Coventry – but I never for one moment thought I would be struggling to get it.

The first heat was becoming something of a complex and as at West Ham in 1969 I failed to score a single point. I came out of the gate like a beginner – and everything else I did on those four laps only reinforced that image.

It was a little wet and while I did get filled in this was no excuse for trailing in last. I just rode badly. The crowd, I think, sensing a sensation, could not have known my anxiety as I went back into the pits.

I was so disgusted with my first race that I thought about changing bikes. Instead I decided to risk it . . . and was taken from the back by Ronnie Moore in my second ride.

Two points from two rides and it began to look as though this might be my last step in the 1970 World Championship. Fellow New Zealander Davey Gifford was in the pits with me and between us we decided to swap bikes for the vital third race.

I had been using the frame on which I had won my two World Finals – I had become somewhat attached to it – and it was a wrench changing over. But it worked and I won my third and fourth races.

I'd got the eight points that I needed – and went out for a fifth time not worrying about where I would finish. It was then that I realised what a funny game speedway was.

Fifteen minutes earlier I had been faced with the frightening thought that I wasn't to go any further. Now, two races later I could throw away a point if I wanted to.

Sjosten added the Nordic/British title to Belle Vue's collection with 14 points while protégé Ole Olsen picked up his first major World championship placing with the runners-up berth that included a victory over me in my fifth outing.

Sjosten, Olsen, Briggo, Ronnie Moore, Jim Airey, Swedes Bengt Jansson and Anders Michanek joined me on the plane trip to Leningrad for the European Final.

At the last minute Jansson dropped out because of a broken wrist and reserve Ove Fundin should have taken his place. Fundin had his own problems with frontier guards at the Russian border so sole Englishman Trevor Hedge found himself in the European Final field – much to his amazement. Indeed it wasn't until after the final that he even realised his points would count and he was ready for his first shot at the World final.

Leningrad was to be an easier meeting than Coventry. Sjosten, Olsen, Briggo, Michanek, Hedge and myself got through and so did Ronnie Moore even though he broke his arm in the process.

In fact of those who qualified from Coventry only Jim Airey failed to get enough points to go a stage further.

I added the European title to the British. And then started to plan for Poland.

There was a longer gap than usual between the European and the World Finals – nearly seven weeks – and during this time I worked myself into the mental state needed to win in Poland.

Now I know that it was a particularly hard time for my wife and family and looking back I can see how they suffered. As week by week went by so my single-minded concentration intensified. I could go days and hardly speak to Raye or the children.

I was building myself into such a mental attitude that one of two things would happen – I would either win the Final or break completely.

I began dropping silly little points in the league and people began wondering if I could really challenge the Poles on their own ground.

I got more and more worked up inside and undoubtedly became harder and harder to live with. It was no easy life for Raye but sensibly she kept a lot of her thoughts to herself and generally stood aside while I carried on in my own far-from-sweet way.

I left for Poland days before the final and spent hours on the practice. I didn't go particularly well and came off once, buckling my back wheel.

With Briggo I practised starts and we both indulged in a little bit of gamesmanship with the Poles and Russians. We would make sure we didn't look *TOO* good.

Mentally I don't think I have ever been so well attuned as I was to winning the title in Poland. There was something so different about it. A strange country. Strange rituals. Strange customs. Strange food.

I knew that my chief opposition would come from two quarters – any one of the Poles. And Briggo. A lot of people had written him off but I still thought he would be the man to beat and I was glad when I saw that we were to meet in the first heat.

Maybe it was a good omen. Hadn't we met in the first heat in my first success in Gothenburg?

The track had altered slightly between practice and final night but it was of no great degree. During practice I had deliberately misled the Poles on one or two little techniques and decided to try and keep the game going right up until the off.

While everyone else hurried about in the pits putting on new tyres I sat comfortably on a box and let everyone believe I wasn't going to put in a new tyre. It wasn't until the parade that mechanics Gordon Stobbs and Chris McDonald actually changed the rear wheel!

If I could have my way I was going to give nothing away at all. The mental pressures I knew were on me. No one had won three titles in a row. If I could I would try and pass on some of those pressures to my opponents.

Once my first heat was over I knew I COULD do it. But it wasn't until my fifth race was over that I knew I HAD done it.

After three unbeaten rides I came up against the in-form Polish favourite Pawel Waloszek who seemed to improve with age. As a youngster he had hardly set the world alight with British club side Coventry but as he reached his thirtieth birthday he matured with each passing year like a good wine.

Waloszek was also unbeaten and as we came to the tapes the baying Poles put up a terrific din completely drowning the few hundred British supporters, including my wife Raye, who had made the trip by charter plane or coach.

Wimbledon's Trevor Hedge had borrowed my bike for the heat. He shouldn't really have ridden following a frightening fall a few heats earlier but he agreed to come to the start – to prevent Poland slotting in their reserve Edmung Migos which would have given the Iron Curtain racers an opportunity to team race.

In the end it didn't matter as I made the finest gate of my 1970 season and cut across to the first bend slightly ahead of Waloszek. He didn't really challenge me and everything rested on heat seventeen.

I was less than eighty seconds away from speedway history. I can't recall my thoughts as I went to the tapes on the black cinder track.

All I remember is that I knew I had to make the most scientifically perfect gate of my life if I was to be a certain winner. If I didn't I still had a chance – but if I did I knew I was there.

Against the tapes, the breeze blowing them into the front wheel, I plotted my course to the vital first bend. The tapes went. And I went. And got there.

Seventy-seven point six seconds later I had crossed the line. The Triple Crown was mine.

Thoughts cascaded through my mind as I made my way back to the pits. I looked in vain for Raye, wanting her to share in my moment of glory. Five minutes later she walked into the pits, the tears streaming down her face, black with the cinder dust.

He white fur coat disfigured with the ugly blackness of the cinders. But that didn't matter. I had done it.

Tension. The tension of weeks of build-up should have disappeared with the lap of honour. It didn't. It was still bottled up inside and after a row with various officials before the after-the-meeting banquet I kissed Raye good-bye as she flew back to Luton on a special charter flight.

I returned the following day on a normal service and spent the next month trying to rid my mind of the psychological hang-ups that produced what I suppose a drug addict would call withdrawal symptoms.

I became moody. Quarrelsome. Raye and I had our arguments and outside the home I became angrier and angrier as little things were built up out of all proportion.

Eventually I saw what was happening – took a break and got back to something like normal life. The pressures, I knew, were over and once again I became a husband and father.

And that made the Wroclaw victory seem even more a joyous occasion.

11

Around the World on a 500 cc Jawa

They made a film *Around the World in Eighty Days*. If they ever want to re-shoot it then I've got a new title . . . *Around the World On a Speedway Bike*.

For that's exactly what it is. I've lost count of the countries that I've visited on my quest for the Triple Crown and I know that but for speedway I wouldn't have seen half the world.

But what is it like riding around the world? To try and answer let me try and take a typical year in my calendar since I won the World Championship.

And there's no better place to start than at the beginning of the year. Usually, in recent seasons I've spent Christmas and the first days of the new year with my family at home in Bramhall, Cheshire.

But within a few days of ringing in the new I'm off on my travels with Australia the first stop.

Take a typical trip Down Under. Sunshine . . . lazy days . . . good friends . . . booze and relaxation. Not too much booze but plenty of everything else.

Believe me everything you see on those *Come to Australia* recruitment films is true. Provided you know where to go. It's not all work.

I'll start at the Sydney Showground and have a couple of outings there. Then over to Adelaide. Maybe back to Sydney and the Liverpool raceway. Brisbane, Queensland. Rockhampton. Ipswich which is about 35 or 40 miles outside Brisbane.

Each track brings back memories. Adelaide where it all started. Sydney and those long drives across with Jack Young. Brisbane, the happy track. Rockhampton and their Olympic size swimming pool. Ipswich? Well, my memory of Ipswich is a little more recent than most. In particular the night I decided to try and go through the card.

Like all Australian tracks Ipswich runs a composite programme with bikes – known Down Under as solos – sidecars and stock or midget cars.

I had five or six rides in the solo section and won them all. Flushed with success I persuaded one of the local drivers to let me pilot his 1,000 c.c. Vincent banked sidecar and won a race; and then drove a stock car and won a stock car race that night. So you can virtually say I cleaned up a meeting!

Also on the same night they had a ladies stock car race and the officials talked Raye, who is quite a good driver, into having a go. She was going quite well for a lap or so but then she got her foot caught under two steel plates under the accelerator.

I'll ride Ipswich on a Wednesday; down to Liverpool (Sydney) on a Friday and up to Brisbane on a Saturday. Perhaps Rockhampton the following Wednesday, Liverpool again on the Friday; Auckland on the Saturday; that was the way it was going until I did about a dozen meetings in Australia with occasional trips to Auckland.

Then I'll catch the plane home to Christchurch to meet up with all the family and friends. Usually we celebrate. Nothing in particular but that's the way we like it in New Zealand.

It becomes more of a holiday as it's speedway once a week at my local track at Templeton although occasionally I'll nip across to North Island for an occasional meeting.

Plenty of barbecues, trips into the country and a regular Friday night trip to the local Christchurch cinema to catch up on the films dominates the New Zealand part of my year which usually lasts until a few weeks before Easter when I am ready to come back to Britain.

In the last couple of seasons I've dropped in at Houston for Class 'C' events – racing on conventional machines with gears, brakes, etc, on a circular, usually quarter mile hard surface circuit – or perhaps the occasional speedway meeting at the tiny 195-yard Costa Mesa track – the most prosperous of the American speedway tracks.

My English season usually begins with a Good Friday challenge match against either Halifax or Sheffield.

Traditionally Belle Vue also run on Easter Saturday and more often than not opponents are fellow Saturday night track Coventry. The reason for this is that as both tracks operate on a Saturday night the speedway fixture has to be fitted into the programme so that there isn't any undue fixture confusion later in the season.

With both tracks running a monthly stock car meeting it is vital that fixture planners work out a convenient date for both clubs.

On Easter Sunday there is always a trip to Germany – usually to Poching which is a little further south than Munich. I come back to England for perhaps the return leg of that challenge with Halifax at The Shay. Then perhaps four or five days further on I'm back at Belle Vue with another German trip on the Sunday.

This is the way it goes through the season with about twenty or more trips to the Continent for Sunday meetings. It is not necessarily Germany, for some weeks I can be riding at Czechoslovakia or Denmark.

To get to Germany I usually get the sleeper train down to London Euston at midnight from Manchester's Piccadilly Station. I'll get out of the train at Euston at about seven in the morning; pick up a couple of Sunday papers and take a taxi the twenty miles or so out to Heathrow and make my way into Terminal Number Two for the European flights.

It gives me time to have a breakfast and read the the newspapers before I catch the plane. I'm usually in the country I am going to ride in by 10-30 or 11 on the Sunday morning.

I have an agent who lives in Germany, Wilfried Drygala, who looks after all my continental bookings and I also leave a couple of bikes with him.

He'll pick me up at the airport in his car with the bikes on a trailer and we have a box on the back of his car with all my spare parts, a helmet, my racing leathers. In fact a complete kit.

Off we go to the track, usually getting there in time to do the compulsory two or three laps practice.

To use a phrase, sometimes the best laid plans of man and mouse go wrong and I have been known to arrive at a meeting with only minutes to spare. Or very occasionally I've rolled into the paddock while the race has been on. That, though, is infrequent and generally fog, mists or the other hazards that can delay an aircraft have been good to me.

Even though practice is compulsory I would try and have a few laps were it not because some of the tracks are about a mile around (the biggest 1½ miles where you can't even see the other side of the track). The fact that you are going to be racing around there at about 100 miles an hour means I ride round a couple of laps to try and spot anything that might cause me trouble.

In Germany the tracks come into two categories usually – a grass track or a sand track. I reckon that if a track has a few blades of grass on it that's a grass track. And if it doesn't that's a sand track.

A lot of people, I'm sure, have the wrong idea about a sand-track and envisage me racing along a beach but that is not the case. It's granite, shale and sand – quite a mixture.

A lot of the tracks are extremely fast – I use a special long track machine built by the Jawa factory with suspension as opposed to the conventional rigid frame of a speedway bike – and extremely bumpy. Obviously more dangerous than a speedway track because of the speeds that you can reach but again the financial rewards are far in excess of anything I can earn on British speedway.

Personally bumps have never bothered me on any track and they don't bother me in Germany although I have had one or two frightening moments when I have come off at something approaching 100 miles an hour. But that's all in the game!

The grass tracks also present their problems because on a wet day they are slippy and some are extremely smooth and extremely fast, particularly Cloppenberg where I have the unofficial world grass track record of 125.8 kilometres an hour for an average lap. Stressing that this is the AVERAGE speed for a lap.

Obviously we have to slow down quite a bit in the middle of the turns so it will give some idea of the speed down the straight. If it has been raining it is definitely dodgy to say the least because it is always terribly slippy and there are usually 12 or 14 riders in each race.

On the other hand a bright sunny day conjures up a dust hazard so either way the grass tracks have got their problems and one or two of them are virtually scrambles tracks.

Kiel is a mile and a half track which is virtually three tracks in one. There is a very fast front straight which is reasonably smooth, there's quite a dangerous corner round by the pits bend (with a hedge on the inside and outside of the track which makes it just like racing down a country lane with a grass-covered road) then there's a really smooth, as smooth as a billiard table, side straight where you go like a rocket at something over 100 miles an hour going into the top corner. Here it's just the opposite. From a smooth fast straight you come into an absolutely incredible stretch with foot-deep ruts. (That makes a rider out of you in about ten yards – otherwise you've finished for the day!)

You come into the third straight which is quite bumpy again before you come back into a reasonably smooth stretch. So you've got a reasonably smooth straight; very dangerous and fast first turn; beautifully fast second straight; an extremely rough corner at the far end, bringing you back along a bumpy straight. As I say the sort of track that will make a rider out of you in two shakes. . . .

One of the other problems is that a lot of the tracks have sidecar racing on the same afternoon and these tend to cut up the track very badly.

Generally the tracks seem to be poles apart. Either they are very good surfaces or as rough as hell.

One of the ideal sand tracks, in shape, size and surface, is Hamburg. I say it's a good track to ride but for two years in succession I've gone end over end at about 90 miles an hour going into the pit corner. The first time I went over there I went past two riders on the outside and the track was so fast that I got the shale from the two bikes I was passing and it literally lifted me off the bike. Both the bike and I went end over end and I finished up in a big heap.

This was just before the World Championship rounds in England and although I didn't get any broken bones I was badly bruised and had bad headaches for a week or so. My bike was like a concertina.

The following year I thought I had learned the lesson and went out by myself to practice and prior to going out I was talking to former World Speedway champion Bjorn Knutsson and was telling him what had happened to me the year before. He told me to take it easy – but what did I do? Going down the front straight at about 100 miles an hour I turned into the bend at full throttle because it is such a beautiful track and hit a bit of a wet patch and came straight down.

Roddenbach is another good track and is a lot smaller than most of the German raceways being only 600 or 700 yards. That's quite a good little track.

A normal season in Germany would mean between 15 and 20 meetings and only two or three of these are the conventional speedway type of meeting. All the others are long-track events.

Sometimes the German commitments can make it rather a hectic time for during one week in 1969 I had a meeting at Munich on Thursday; Glasgow on Friday; Belle Vue on Saturday; Frankfurt on the Sunday.

Because I do so little speedway in Germany I don't keep a speedway bike over there but for these two particular meetings I needed a bike. I had to have my car over there and as it happened this week coincided with school holidays so Raye drove over with me and we had something of a holiday. A couple of days after the Frankfurt meeting I had the World Best Pairs at Malmo in Sweden and the following night an open meeting at Norkopping so it made quite an unusual trip.

Most of the meetings in Germany are annual events run by the clubs attached to the local track and even though some of the towns are very small they attract crowds of about 20,000 with people coming from miles around.

It means that I have virtually a yearly schedule in Germany and because of the big crowds and the fact that it is a once-a-year occasion the clubs can pay at least several hundred pounds to have me ride.

So far I've only ridden in West Germany although every year a number of East German clubs ask me to take part in their meetings.

Most of the meetings in Germany are run with three qualifying races from which the top six in each that go into a final. The rider who wins the final is the overall winner no matter how he has finished in a heat. Usually I only race three or four times an afternoon and after the meeting – they always seem to drag on with bands playing, people dancing: a general carnival atmosphere – it is usually seven or seven-thirty before we leave the track.

Wherever I ride, unless it is near Munich, we go back to Bremen and I stay at Wilfried's home and get the early morning flight back to London Airport and catch a connection to Manchester and am usually back in the house expecting a cup of tea and something to eat at about mid-day.

From practically anywhere in Europe I can usually get back to Manchester by mid-day on the Monday so while it sounds as if I am spending a lot of time away from home it isn't quite as much as it sounds. In fact, a trip to Germany and back is probably as easy for me as the long drive up to Glasgow or down to Exeter.

And it has one big advantage – most of the time I am able to relax either in the plane or with Wilfrid driving the car.

Besides racing regularly in Germany I also made sorties into Czechoslovakia on two counts. One to ride at meetings such as the famous two day Golden Helmet meeting at Pardubice and to visit the Jawa factory in Prague.

I have to go there first of all at Easter to collect my bikes for speedway and the long-track and generally to have a chat to the factory bosses about any new developments they may have on the machine.

I drive from Czechoslovakia up through Germany and drop all my Continental equipment at Wilfried's so that it is handily based within reach of all the tracks I will ride at.

I take a trailer with me and pile all the bikes on it although I usually make at least another two or three trips to the factory to pick up new bikes or more spares.

Speedway in Czechoslovakia has undoubtedly improved in recent seasons and I see them coming more and more into world class competition so I expect to make more trips behind the Iron Curtain as the years go by.

To talk of going to Czechoslovakia for a couple of hours' racing may sound something of a waste of time but despite its Communist background Czecho is in fact as accessible as most western countries.

I can leave home at about six o'clock in the morning and catch the mid-day ferry from Dover to Ostend and drive from Ostend to Prague.

If I drive by myself – my mechanic Guy Allott has been over with me – I can stop at one of the road-houses on the Autobahn for a sleep for a couple of hours and can then drive into Prague at something like 6.30 on the Monday morning – a road trip of something like 24 hours. I always stay at the same motel on the way into Prague and snatch a couple of hours sleep before driving out to the factory in the afternoon.

The factory is, in fact, about 45 miles outside Prague and usually everything is waiting for me so I stay the night in Prague and then head back on the Tuesday driving back via Bremen before coming back to England.

Wilfried can also nip down to Prague for me if anything urgent is needed and he takes virtually complete control of my continental career. He owns a large trucking company in Germany and at one end of the depot where they service the trucks there is a small bay which has been furnished inside purely to house my long-track bikes.

One of his truck mechanics, a motor-cycle racing enthusiast, looks after my bike during the week and makes sure that the chains are oiled, the clutch washed out, changing the gear ratio for the following week and changing the tyres round.

So from Sunday to Sunday the only real work that I need to do on the bike is if something big has gone wrong with it that day in which case when we get back to Wilfried's after the meeting we go into the workshop and swap engines and I bring the parts that need repairing back with me in the airport bag, giving them to Guy Allott who finds out what has gone wrong in his workshop at Buxton. Guy will repair them and I will take them back the following week.

Basically the only things I need to do before I ride is the final clutch adjustment; the final chain adjustment; the final tyre pressure gauge work and those little things that need my personal attention.

Of course every meeting doesn't go off at a smooth rate and there have been times when I've been forced to do more than usual.

Generally speaking though it is easier for me to ride in Germany on a Sunday than it is to ride in England during the week – without taking into consideration the financial side of it.

One of the strangest trips I have ever made must have been during the winter of 1966–1967 when I decided to go . . . ice-racing.

I was somewhat bored with doing very little and waiting for the 1967 speedway season to come around when it was brought to my attention that the Russians had been granted the World Ice Racing Championship and in order that they could call it a World championship they had to have representatives from other countries.

Naturally no one in England was going to be interested in going to Russia to race on ice if it was going to cost them money but I really fancied it as a bit of experience and as the Russians had offered our Control Board enough money to cover the expenses of two riders and a manager I was very interested in going.

At one stage it looked as if I would be the only rider going and it didn't really seem as if I would have a manager. No one seemed to be very interested in going to Russia for one thing – shades of Siberia and all that – and secondly no one seemed too keen to chance riding on ice.

However one night I was with another New Zealander, Goog Allan from Hamilton, who was living along the road from us and we were talking about it. I told him I was going and where I was going; what time I had to leave; what time I would be in Siberia and so on and before the evening was out he had turned round and said: 'If they'll let me I'll come with you.'

The familiar black and white checked crash helmet is readily recognisable as that which masks a World Champion

It's not often I get behind the wheel of a car like this. But I enjoyed this drive at a sponsored meeting at Belle Vue

Racing round the world. *Left:* Travelling partner to the World Ice-Speedway Championship in Siberia was fellow Kiwi Goog Allan. Note those fearsome looking spikes! *Below:* I dive under American National Champion Rick Woods at Costa Mesa, California

He asked me to ring up Mr John McNulty, secretary of the Speedway Control Board, to ask if he could join me as Britain's second rider. The next morning I made the call and Mr McNulty turned round and said: 'Of course. The money's here for two riders and a team manager – we might as well use it.'

That meant two New Zealanders were going to represent Britain. About a week later Mr McNulty phoned up and said that Trevor Redmond had been in that day and he had got very interested in it and it ended up that Trevor would go as our manager!

So within six or seven days what had looked like a lonely one man trip had been re-arranged into what was a New Zealand benefit with Goog as my partner and another New Zealander as team manager!

Off we went from the West London Air Terminal early one morning out to Heathrow to get the plane to Moscow. We got into Moscow and waited around for a while during which time the Russian Motor Federation were very, very good to us taking us round and showing us the sights of Moscow.

We were there a couple of days before we set out by train for Siberia by the Trans-Siberian Railway. As most people, I'd only ever heard of the legendary Siberian salt-mines and I had no real idea what to expect as we trundled across the wide expanses of the Soviet Union.

I know that the journey took something like 55 hours. Really though it was quite a pleasant journey because the train was quite luxurious with air conditioning. Apart from the food which we found putrid – we couldn't eat it and had to go on to our cracker biscuits! – we really enjoyed the trip.

We had the West German representatives in the next cabin to us and the Swedish team was a little further on so we all got to know each other and had quite a good trip.

We arrived at Novasibersk and the following day we had to go out and practice. It wasn't only our first riding experience on ice – it was the first time we had even seen it.

One really imagines ice-racing as something absolutely fantastic and an incredible spectacle but in fact it is nowhere near as exciting to watch as regular speedway.

The machines differ in a number of respects with the most noticeable change being in tyres. Instead of the treaded speedway tyres they are covered in spikes to get grip on the ice surface.

The riders, too, look completely different as extra padding, particularly on the knee and backside, is the order of the day.

I was first out in practice and I know I wasn't going very fast but I was enjoying it. As I came back in a Swedish friend Evert Andersson gave me a few pointers saying I wasn't getting the bike down low enough and that I was to almost touch the left handlebar on the ice as I went into the corner.

I tried to put what he had told me into practice and I started to go faster and faster but I think I must have got a bit too cocky because I went into one corner and actually touched the handlebar on the ice which lifted the front wheel off the ice. This meant I lost adhesion and away the bike went.

Strangely, when you fall off you seem to increase speed and I just kept sliding until I hit the crash barrier on the outside of the track. There's nothing to stop you because you just slide across the ice into the barrier.

I think it was a normal speedway track in the summer but because of the cold and snow it had been converted into an ice-raceway. The snow is smoothed out and freezes hard and they just brush the top surface against the wooden safety fence but they don't smooth it off so it forms a rough ice wall.

To mark the inside of the track they line it with a purple, emulsion type indelible ink which is about three inches wide but it is easily seen because everything else is white.

Goog, also on his first trip, seemed to get the hang of it straight away and was going pretty well in the practice. So much so that one of the Russian organisers came to our hotel that evening and was quite enthusiastic about Goog's performance.

As to the meeting itself we rode in two separate semi-finals which meant that if we qualified we went straight into the World Final which struck me as being a little unfair to the Eastern bloc riders who had had to ride a series of qualifying rounds to get to the semi-final stage whereas two complete novices were able to get there without ever having ridden on ice before.

I think this proved that we were only there to make up another country so that it could legitimately be called a World Final although at the time I did feel rather proud to have reached the semi-final of the World Ice-Racing Championship!

We certainly weren't there with any hope of winning anything and we were probably keeping two riders who might have had a chance of winning the title out of the meeting. But it was not ours to reason why – more so in the middle of Siberia.

That's the way it goes in any sport and I suppose the Kenyans may have other runners capable of winning an Olympic 1500 metre title but because they don't happen to be among the country's top two they are kept out of it.

What amazed us in particular about our first impressions of ice-racing was how difficult it was for us to walk around the pit area. Everything was icy and we had difficulty even walking around and yet the Russians could actually run along and push-start their bikes on it. Another point about it was that each country had its own little centrally-heated workshop which meant riding straight off the track into a workshop rather than riding into a central area.

We couldn't possibly start the bikes ourselves – we couldn't run along – so the Russians had to do it for us . . . and they seemed quite happy and helpful.

We had the first meeting on the Saturday and we all had to march around in a big parade as we would for a speedway meeting and Goog and I were in trouble.

While the Russians and other competitors could walk around on the inside of the speedway track, Goog, Trevor and I, had to walk with one foot over the other on the purple painted line which was a little bit abrasive giving us some grip.

All the others were walking apparently without difficulty, while we could hardly keep our balance! One of the surprising things was that even though we were 25 degrees below freezing some days we didn't seem to feel the cold. The snow was just like dry sand and not even wet enough for us to make snowballs to throw at each other. It appeared to be very dry and we couldn't believe it when they told us what the daily temperature was.

In the first meeting I got one point and Goog did a lot better scoring about seven which, considering it was the first time he had ever ridden, was a remarkable performance. We hadn't expected to do very well, and to be frank I didn't find the races as interesting to watch as speedway. There wasn't a lot of passing and it seemed that there was such a difference of standard of riders that in a lap the four riders would be spread over half a lap distance.

This may have been something of a misconception on my part because we were watching a big meeting and maybe the general league racing in Sweden or Russia is far closer and exciting but the two meetings I saw were far from being the exciting spectacle I had originally expected.

The following day was the second semi-final and the Russians seemed delighted that Goog had scored seven points and appeared to think that he should definitely qualify for the final as it would be a good crowd draw when the finals were held in Moscow and Leningrad if there was a British rider in the final.

The place was buzzing with excitement on the Saturday night alive with the fact that Goog was going to qualify. However, on the Sunday Goog only got about three points and he failed to reach the final.

Nevertheless he did superbly well and I honestly think he was far keener on the sport than I was. In fact he was so enthusiastic that he went back the following year and was a near certain finalist when he was involved in an accident which landed him in a Russian hospital for a week. He injured a knee and it never really healed 100 per cent so Goog never got into the final although his partner in 1968, Andy Ross, was eventually to finish fifth in the 1970 final.

So I can claim to have been in on the ground floor of what quickly became a genuine British challenge in ice-racing circles.

Another vivid memory of this particular trip – my first to the Soviet Union – was on the Sunday night when the meeting was over – we had a huge banquet and everyone seemed to get drunk on vodka.

All sorts of people stood up to give speeches and for some unknown reason during the speech (of course I couldn't understand what was being said) everyone would throw back a glass of vodka. The empty glass would be immediately filled up by a waiter and there would be a toast for something else. Vodka was flowing like water and by the end of the banquet everyone was decidedly the worse for drink.

We stayed over for a few days and then went back to Moscow by air before flying back to England. While I would never contemplate making the trip for ice-racing again it is definitely a trip that will always have a place in my memories.

While that was my first trip to Russia – and a trip in which I saw Siberia at its worst in the middle of the winter – I have made other trips to the Soviet Union.

A few years later I went to Leningrad with my club team Belle Vue for a mini-tour as part of the town-linking celebrations between Manchester and Leningrad.

Besides allowing me to see Leningrad in the autumn I also had an opportunity to make my first visit to Finland. It came about because the Belle Vue team left Manchester on the Sunday and drove across Sweden having crossed the North sea by ferry to Gothenburg.

I was to fly from Prague where I had business to join the team for a meeting against a Stockholm side on the Tuesday night. My plane was delayed and I didn't arrive in Stockholm until about eleven o'clock at night which meant that I missed the meeting. However on the Wednesday I travelled with the Belle Vue team to Helsinki and then on down to Leningrad. I found the trip very interesting; the Belle Vue boys were a great bunch and we had a laugh all the way.

One thing I won't forget about this jaunt is the fishing trip. Morris Marshall, who was at that time general manager of Belle Vue; Dent Oliver the Belle Vue speedway manager; and our Swedish rider Soren Sjosten are very keen anglers.

In Finland there are scores of lakes and rivers that make ideal spots for fishing. We came across one just off the road, and the cavalcade – we had two cars and a truck with all the bikes – pulled into the side.

There was a big notice showing a sketch of a man fishing in the river with Swedish and Finnish writing underneath the notice. As no one else could read either language we asked Soren what it meant and he said it was a fishing spot.

Mr Marshall, Mr Oliver and Soren, wearing big grins, got out their fishing rods and went fishing while the rest of us had a good look round the woods for an hour or two while they settled down to a spot of fishing.

Eventually we all got back into the car and a couple of miles down the road Soren started laughing to himself.

It wasn't until we got somewhere near the Finnish/Russian border that Soren turned round to Mr Marshall and asked: 'Do you want to know what that sign really said?'

Then he tossed his head back and laughed: 'It really said if anyone is caught fishing here they will go to jail for 28 days without any trial!'

Once we were in Leningrad we were feted by the local Neva club who booked us in at Leningrad's top hotel and they made sure that we saw all the sights of the city. Instead of coming back by road I had arranged to fly back to Manchester with Soren and another Belle Vue director Mr Jack Fearnley.

And we had quite a scare on that trip. We were scheduled to stop at Amsterdam overnight but the fog came down in an unpenetrable screen but our pilot still went down.

He must have been within a few feet of touching down when he suddenly opened the throttle and went into a steep climb. Apparently he was told not to land at the last moment and we went on to Brussels.

My next trip to Russia was for the 1970 European Final in Leningrad. We were due to fly from Gatwick to Helsinki where the Russians had arranged to fly us down to Leningrad.

For some reason or another it took about eight or nine hours to fly over to Helsinki and the plane must have been just about the first plane built after the Wright Brothers. And it was one of the most uncomfortable trips I have ever spent because besides all the British based qualifiers we had more than a dozen bikes, spare wheels, engines and everything packed into this tiny plane that seemed to be having a job keeping in the sky.

On the way back it had been arranged that we would go back to Helsinki by train before boarding a plane. And that train trip was also to prove quite eventful.

After such an important meeting we all relaxed and no one felt like sleeping that night. I think most of us had had a bit too much vodka to drink and generally there was a riotous time going on with singing and shouting.

All of which culminated in the Finnish police wanting to eject one of the riders from the train because he was making so much noise that the other passengers couldn't get to sleep.

It was only after we had pleaded with the guards to let us take care of him that he was allowed back on the train and we were able to continue the journey.

Before this, however, the Russian customs officials had got on to the train and had inspected everyone's money to see how it compared to the financial statement that you have to give to customs officials before you enter most Iron Curtain countries.

You have to sign a declaration stating how much money you have going into the country and must still have this declaration when you come out. You also have to explain what has happened to the money you took in with you.

We had all been paid for the meeting and for various things which had been sold to the Iron Curtain riders. Even though it didn't amount to a lot of money the Russian officials were very wary of it all and there was a lot of arguing going on.

The Russian officials couldn't get any real sense out of us as we tried to explain what had happened and one of our party in particular spent a long time trying to explain how he came to have so much money with him.

At one time it looked as if we would all end up spending the night in a Russian prison but luckily for us we passed over the Finnish border where the Russian guards had to get off the train.

It wasn't the end of our trouble though, because when we got to Helsinki we found that our bikes weren't, as had been expected, on the train and that they wouldn't be coming until some hours later. We had to tell the charter pilots the sad news which caused even more complications because they could only fly out at certain times and they had to have a break between duties. As a result we had to wait in Helsinki until late evening before we could fly out.

Financially the trip was a disaster for everyone who went over to Leningrad. I came back as European Champion – and with my point, start and prize money I made about £86 out of the trip.

The problems we had flying to and from Helsinki brings back memories of other plane trips I have made since returning to England in 1963. And of occasions when I crossed my fingers and trusted to luck that I'd get through in one piece.

It might sound a little strange coming from someone used to dicing with death at 100 mile an hour to say that I'm not so keen on aeroplane trips. But that's the truth. I don't mind being comfortably settled back in a VC10 or something of that size but when it comes down to something smaller I'm definitely not too keen. The end of the journey can't come quick enough for me.

At odd times going to tracks well off the beaten track as far as BOAC or any of the other national airlines are concerned, I've often had to charter small planes to make sure I got there.

Three trips really come to mind. The first of these was when Danish Champion Ole Olsen – a youngster I virtually discovered at the Belle Vue winter training sessions and who I then fixed up with a team place at Newcastle – and I had a meeting a few miles from Ole's hometown Haderslev in Denmark.

In order to get there in time for the meeting we had to charter a plane from Ringway Airport, Manchester. And the only plane available for charter was a tiny four-seater!

As we had to pay for the plane anyway we asked around to see if anyone else wanted to come across with us and in the end two New Zealanders, Dave Gifford and Bill Moulin said they'd like to come.

Going over there we noticed that the fuel gauge was nearly empty as we got half way across. We all looked down and all we could see was cloud. Under that we all knew was a long, long drop into the North Sea. And looking around I could see the tension building up in the faces of Ole, Dave and Bill. Inside I was becoming increasingly worried as the gauge slowly slid past the empty pointer. Mentally I was beginning to rehearse the ditching procedure and I knew that similar thoughts were rushing through the minds of my travelling companions.

But we all put on a brave face and no one would mention the fact. You could feel the tense atmosphere in the plane as all conversation stopped.

Then came what we had all been dreading . . . the cough, the splutter and the silence as the engine stopped.

I braced myself as I expected the nose-dive down into the drink as the plane started to shake. I was certain we were on our way down and from the look in the eyes of the other boys so were they.

Then coolly the pilot took over. Stretched across . . . flicked a switch . . . and we went on to a reserve tank that none of us had realised was there!

A gasp of realisation . . . and conversation started up again!

The second incident was when Barry Briggs and I were hopping across Europe for one of our regular jaunts to compete in a meeting at Pardubice in Czechoslovakia.

One again we chartered a four-seater plane and at the last minute the Czech promoters asked if we could take two other riders with us. After a hasty search around we asked Eddie Reeves, then captain of Oxford, and his team-mate Rick Timmo if they wanted to come with us.

We were due to leave Gatwick at about 5.30 a.m. on the Sunday morning so after riding at Belle Vue I travelled down there; Barry drove across from Swindon where he had a meeting; and the two boys joined us at Gatwick.

A thick blanket of fog covered the runways and it was obvious we weren't going to be able to take off on schedule. We settled back in the lounge having coffee, lunch and reading a few Sunday papers as time dragged on.

We knew that if we left by one o'clock we still had a chance of getting to the meeting. As the fog started to lift we all went on board. The pilot, though, had mislaid the key to the plane's hold and we had to take all our luggage on to the plane and stack it at the nose end. What we couldn't put there we had to carry with us.

Once we got into the air the plane seemed to be perpetually pointing towards the ground, no doubt because of the luggage in the nose. Throughout the trip we held on to our seats, clutching our hand luggage, convinced that the plane was about to go into a nose-dive crashing to the ground.

Because of this it took us an hour and a half longer than usual to get to Prague and by the time we were driven to Pardubice the meeting was over. So all Barry and I did was to drive around the track waving to the fans . . . without even riding in a proper race.

We took a lot of ragging over that as the Czechs found it pretty funny that we had just popped in for a cup of coffee so to speak!

On another occasion I had to ride at Stavanger, Norway, with three top Swedes, Ove Fundin, Torbjorn Harryson and Bengt Jansson.

It was the day after the 1967 British League Riders Final. Once the meeting was over we rushed across to Manchester Airport straight after the meeting and found our plane waiting for us.

It looked such a frail, light thing that we all staged a stay-at-home strike and told the pilot that we couldn't go with him until it was daylight.

Not one of us was willing to risk a night flight over to Norway in a plane that size. The pilot wasn't very happy about that and got on the phone to the Norwegian Motor Federation to see if they could make us change our minds.

But no matter what they said the four of us had made up our minds . . . we definitely weren't going in that plane until daybreak. We sat around the deserted airport arguing with the pilot as he tried everything he knew to convince us that it would be an uneventful trip and that it was vital he took off during darkness.

We wouldn't be swayed and in the end he had to reluctantly accept that we meant it when we said we weren't getting into the plane. Finally dawn broke and an hour or so later we agreed to get on board as we took off for Stavanger.

And I can honestly say that after all the trouble we had just about the smoothest day-time flight ever! And once we arrived at Stavanger we knew why there had been all the panic.

The same pilot and plane were due to leave Stavanger to fly down to Copenhagen to pick up actor Roger 'The Saint' Moore who was to open the meeting and drive round a lap of honour in his famous Volvo car.

Obviously the plane was late and he turned out to be the interval attraction as the meeting was well under way by the time he was dropped off at Stavanger!

12

Problems, Problems, Problems

Undoubtedly one of the most publicised periods in my career was when I was at loggerheads with my Newcastle promoter Mike Parker.

Thousands of words have been written about our long lasting dispute but there is still so much that remained hidden from the public.

Before I embark on telling the complete story of the breakdown of our working arrangement I must say that I accept a lot of the blame for it.

It certainly wasn't a case of my being wronged all along the line. Many things happened during our tempestuous partnership and I dare say that if we had our time again things might be different.

Or they might be the same, for basically we were both independent characters and it was this rather than any other single factor that caused all the trouble.

To begin the story I have to go back to 1963 when I came back for my second spell in England. Mike had cabled that he was willing to pay not only my boat fare but also that of my wife and our children.

That was something that no other promoter in England seemed eager to do and no matter what happens in my relationship with Mr Parker I will always be grateful to him for that.

Throughout 1963 he gave me considerable help and I had no real complaints about my treatment. It was his willingness to help me during that first year that convinced me I ought to stay with Newcastle during 1964 – the year the Provincial League went black.

At the beginning of the 1964 season Mike had told me that the domestic dispute between the Provincial League and the National League would be resolved by June and that I would have a chance to ride in the World Championship.

This never in fact came about but I accept – and never doubted – that Mike had been sincere in his belief that the problems would be sorted out and I realised it was through no fault of his that I missed the entire 1964 World Championship.

Up until a few days before the qualifying rounds were raced I had the opportunity to transfer to a licensed National League track – it would have meant I could ride in the rounds – but I still felt my allegiance was with Newcastle.

As it turned out it meant only one season in unlicensed speedway for both leagues got together and the all-embracing British League was launched in 1965.

Again I stayed with Newcastle – and again I had no qualms about doing so. We were getting on as well as any employer-employee relationship.

The first real rift in our friendship came during the 1966 season when I qualified for my first World Final – held that year in the Swedish sea-port of Gothenburg at the striking Ullevi Stadium.

Having won the European Final at Wembley I felt some confidence about my chances in the final. Perhaps I was expecting too much but I took it for granted that I would be allowed to go to the pre-meeting practice which that year was held on the Wednesday before the Friday night final.

I began preparing to go, and to take everything I needed I had to leave England by ferry on the Monday. That meant asking permission to miss the Monday evening meeting at Newcastle and I took it that that would be a mere formality.

But much to my surprise Newcastle were apparently not prepared to allow me to miss the Brough Park meeting.

My first reaction was that I would catch that Monday ferry – and to hell with the meeting. It was then pointed out that if I did so there was a possibility I might be suspended.

So I had no option. I couldn't risk a suspension on the eve of my World Final debut so I rode at Newcastle. But inwardly I knew that this was what would make me leave the track – no matter how long it took.

Little did I realise that it was going to take another three years before I could get away. Mike did suggest that I fly over to Gothenburg on the Wednesday so that I would still be able to have the practice and fulfil my commitments to Newcastle.

It sounded a good idea. It would have meant going on a regular

BEA flight and I found that I could only take one bike and very little else.

As far as I was concerned that was no good. I wanted to take spare gears, spare wheels, spare tyres – in fact everything. After giving it a lot of thought I decided I would be better off *NOT* going on the Wednesday as I might get a false impression of the track if I only had one machine.

Unless I was going to be able to try different gears and different tyres I honestly believed it would serve no useful purpose. I was afraid that to spend a couple of hours practising on one bike, with one gear range and one cut back tyre might work against me on final night.

Even at this stage I wanted to fly over on the Thursday and walk around the track and have a good look at it the day before the final. But I couldn't get my bikes and gear flown over by BEA because they only had regular flights every second day so as it turned out I wouldn't have been able to go.

Eventually the only way I could get over was on a charter flight arranged by supporters! So I set off for my first world final on a charter flight not having had a practice or a look at the track I was going to ride on. Hardly the professional way of tackling such a big meeting.

I wasn't alone though, for three other finalists were also on the charter flight – Mike Broadbanks, Nigel Boocock and reserve Ken McKinlay. These three riders had ridden at Gothenburg in previous years so at least they had seen the track – which was more than I had done!

Eventually we arrived at Gothenburg during Friday afternoon only a few hours before the meeting was due to start. What a way to prepare for a final! We were only allowed one bike each on the flight and a few tools, spares, gears, tyres, etc.

Compare this to the way the Poles and Russians arrived – with teams of mechanics and a battery of spare bikes, what seemed like scores of tyres, and a virtual factory of spares.

I felt very much the poor relation of the final (as must all the English boys who were also restricted in the way I was) and wasn't even able to have a mechanic with me.

Anyway I looked at the track and decided what gear I felt I should be pulling. I watched the first couple of races and the straights looked much longer when the four riders were on the track. This made me decide to have a higher gear so while I was on two minutes for my first ride in my first world final Ken McKinlay and Mike Broadbanks helped me change gear and I went higher.

I knew once the race started that I had made the wrong decision and I was beaten by Norwegian Sverre Harrfeldt who went on to get second place dropping his only point to winner Barry Briggs.

Having had my first race in heat three I was out again in heat five so I didn't have time to change gear, spending the few minutes in between brushing the dirt off the front and back wheels, generally cleaning where I could reach and filling the fuel tanks with methanol and oil.

So I went into my second race half knowing I was using the wrong gear but unable to change it. I dropped another two points – this time to Pole Antoni Woryna and Russian Igor Plechanov so after two rides I had only three points and any hopes I might have had of winning the title on my debut had gone.

After heat five I had a long gap before my third ride in heat eleven and I got myself composed, changed to the right gear and was ready to go into battle again.

In my last three races I won two heats and came second in the other to Bee-Bee so I finished with eight points from my last three rides dropping my only point to the eventual champion who went through the card undefeated.

I honestly felt that had I had the right gear for my first two rides I might have been able to get at least another two points from those starts which would have been enough to give me third place at least. And had I beaten Harrfeldt in my first race I could have finished second. But all that was pure conjecture and while I believed it myself I obviously have no direct evidence that it would have happened.

It may have been I would have scored the same points with the right gear on. The important thing was that I didn't think so – and even more important I blamed my late arrival for it.

I certainly felt that by robbing me of the chance of practice it had also robbed me of a possible second place in the World Final. I felt I hadn't been given a fair chance.

During the winter of 1966 and 1967 I spoke to Mike about the possibility of a transfer although I never made an official request to move from Newcastle.

I was living in a flat he owned only a couple of doors away from his office in Upper Chorlton Road, Manchester, so we had plenty of time to talk to each other.

It was also around about this time that we first had any disagreement over money. Up until then I'd always been satisfied with the money I had been receiving.

To explain, under the rules of speedway a rider is really only entitled to what he earns out on the track. In reality this never works and virtually every top-class rider in the country receives what is basically an illegal payment.

These 'under-the-counter' payments are so rife in British speedway that to try and stop them would throw the sport into chaos. It is, after all, only natural that a man should ask for what he considers he is worth.

They take various forms and even the simple act of giving a man his fare to come to England can be, according to the rule-book, an illegal payment.

I believe that at that time promoters were allowed to pay a maximum of £250 in fares to an Australian rider but most paid well over the top.

Having won the European Championship and having finished fourth in the World Final I considered that I was worth more than Mike was prepared to pay me!

We moved into the 1967 season with Newcastle still my league team – and with two main troubles hovering around. One was my inability to compete in the '66 practice. The other – money.

Although we still disagreed over money I agreed to stay at Newcastle for the season and Mike agreed to buy me a brand new Jawa to use for the season, as well as a cash agreement we had.

Unfortunately, and through no fault of Mike's the bike was a proper lemon. Almost from the beginning of the season things began to go wrong with the bike and although Mike had several expert mechanics look after it, it just refused to react to all known engine standards. Everything was technically correct with the machine and it baffled men of considerable mechanical knowledge as it refused to respond as it should have done.

This didn't particularly bother me because I was mainly a Jap man anyway and I only wanted the Jawa to ride on what I considered to be scramble tracks. Basically the reason for this is that the Jawa was better for a rough track than the reliable Jap although there is very little between the two of them.

Whenever I was on a track I considered to be a true speedway circuit, smooth and with a good surface, I would ride the Jap.

Mike and I argued a lot in private during 1967, but sometimes it came out into the open.

During the months of June and July things really blew up as I had trouble after trouble with my bikes and nothing that I did seemed to improve the engines, particularly that Jawa I had been given.

A sign of our deteriorating partnership at Newcastle was what the Newcastle fans were reading in their programme.

In Eddie Glennon's *Seeing Speedway* column, for example, on 3rd July he wrote: 'Half the battle in speedway is the preparation of the engine, and it is each rider's responsibility to provide and maintain his own equipment. Normally most riders do a grand job on this score but sometimes a man runs into snags which build up into a cumulative total of despair, and he reaches the point where he begins to think when things will go right. This is what is happening to our skipper (that was me) right now.

'He has spent more time and cash in his efforts to get going than any other rider I know, and in desperation last week we asked Dave Younghusband's father Joe, who is a top mechanic, to have a go and see if he could cure it. We all saw the result.

'Now Ivan, because he knows he should be going better, gets very emotional about this and we saw signs of this last Monday. But before you all start writing letters to the paper let me remind you of that match winning ride in heat 13 on a borrowed bike. This is the test of a skipper – win the match first and give up afterwards if that's how he feels. We do not like to see any rider showing temperament in public, but we are big enough to realise the strain he is under trying to live up to his reputation and being constantly thwarted by the gremlins.'

That was the prelude to one of the stormiest sessions in my career up to then.

Against Wolverhampton on 26th June the Jawa again seized solid and I had to borrow bikes to finish the meeting. A few days later I was at Sheffield for Newcastle so took my Jap along as Owlerton has long been recognised as one of the smoothest tracks in the country. Here my troubles returned and I dropped a valve. It was the second consecutive night on which I had had trouble with my bikes and I felt really sick.

I was so fed up at this stage that, rightly or wrongly, I told Mike

Two champions together – five times No. 1, Ove Fundin, and Triple Crown holder Ivan Mauger

ₐnd again! This time I ake tennis star Rod ͺaver on a lap of ͺonour at Australia's ꞦRockhampton track in ꞦSeptember, 1962

In thirteen seasons of speedway, I've made many friends and ridden with hundreds of different riders. First time in Britain, my Eastbourne team-mate was Colin 'Joe' Goody (*above left*); later I teamed up with Brian Craven (*above right*) when he was captaining Newcastle. Belle Vue colleague Soren Sjosten (*right*) provided many a laugh on two trips to Russia

Parker he would have to get me a bike if he wanted me to ride on the Saturday night in a league match at Swindon.

As far as I was concerned I was going to retire until the bikes were in a good condition. Although Mike wasn't under any obligation to help riders with their bikes I think he could see my mental state at that time and sensing my exasperation he agreed to get me a bike.

However the Jap spare engine he got for me wasn't up to what I considered to be my standard. I went out in the first heat and gated ahead of everyone else. Barry Briggs passed me down the back straight which wasn't so unusual because he usually passed most people at Swindon! But then his second string passed me and so did my own team partner.

By this time I was completely choked and rode on to the grass and once the race was over I kept the engine running and rode straight through the pits and out to my car. Five minutes later I was in the showers and I'd left the stadium before the first half had even ended.

My actions were wrong and against the rule-book, and I must say that although the bike was not as good as I hoped the Newcastle promotion had made an effort to get it for me. They had also borrowed a Jawa from a junior for me to ride at Swindon, but I didn't want to know anything about it.

It is hard to explain one's emotions and why you do something like this, but all I can say is that mentally I was completely fed up with things going wrong.

Again the matter was fully aired in the Newcastle programme and Eddie Glennon finished his column with the words: 'I am sorry about the whole unpleasant incident – but life is not easy all the time and one must learn to take the rough with the smooth. I think Ivan is man enough to sort out his troubles and ride himself back to where he belongs, right at the top.'

And behind the scenes our arguments and disagreements continued. Basically I suppose that Mike is a determined man and so am I.

By now it was general knowledge that I wanted to get away from Newcastle and throughout the winter of 1967 I had promoters on the phone offering me inducements to join them for the following season.

Several promoters made offers to me to ride for them in '68 and the offers went from £500 at the bottom of the scale to a house at the top. In the middle were all sorts of bait dangled in front of me including bikes and cars.

And who said there were no illegal payments in British speedway?

Due to a number of circumstances I wasn't able to get a transfer during the winter.

At the beginning of 1968 I was in a position where I either rode for Newcastle or I couldn't ride anywhere in Britain. I chose Newcastle!

By this time I was officially third in the world and with the final going to be in Sweden again in 1968 I definitely didn't relish the thought of being associated with Newcastle at that time.

Our relationship was running at a very low ebb and it was definitely under protest that I lined up in Newcastle's colours. I knew I was going home at the end of 1968 no matter what happened during the year, no matter what, I definitely wouldn't have come back to ride for Mike Parker in 1969. So I knew that at the worst I would have to spend only six months or so as one of his riders.

I think we both accepted that we couldn't patch up our difference and several of our arguments made big news in the Newcastle papers and the Speedway press.

All were of little significance until once again we came round to the month of June which always seemed to be the time for a real blow-up. Perhaps the fact that it was virtually mid-way through the season had something to do with it. I was riding for Great Britain at Wolverhampton on Friday, 21st June and had something of a disastrous night.

The following night I was at Coatbridge in another test match and again I had engine trouble. I only scored three points as Britain were massacred by the Swedes who topped seventy points.

Before flying off to Germany that night from Glasgow I telephoned Raye and when she asked me what had gone wrong with the bike I said I didn't know but that it could possibly have been a bad connection with the spark plugs and that I would check it on Monday when I got back from Germany.

During the Sunday a newspaper reporter phoned my wife and asked her what the fault had been and Raye, not being a mechanically-minded person, said that I had told her it might have been a plug.

When I arrived at Newcastle on the Monday I picked up the evening paper and read an article which included a statement by my promoter. My interpretation of it was that I didn't work properly on my bikes and didn't even have the inclination to change a spark plug.

This was a bit too much for me to take after working until the early morning on many nights trying to make sure my bikes were mechanically perfect. Often I would arrive back home at Manchester at two or three in the morning after a meeting and stay in the garage for a couple of hours fixing things before going to bed.

I hit back by telling a reporter I knew on the morning *Newcastle Journal* a lot of the things I had been thinking – mainly that the Newcastle track was like a scrambles course and that I would be better off riding a scrambles or trials bike on it than a speedway bike.

After this bust-up I decided that I would ride out the rest of the season at Newcastle – but that would be it. I would willingly have moved to another track if I had been allowed to but I wasn't and I stuck it out mainly because the World Final was approaching.

That Monday at Newcastle was certainly one of the most incredible days I have spent in speedway. Besides my verbal bust up with the promoter I also staged my own sit-down strike after being excluded by the referee for breaking the time limit.

I resigned the captaincy of the Newcastle team and made it quite plain to anyone who would listen that once my contract finished so did my Newcastle days.

I think people may have thought a lot of what I said in those days was little more than an idle threat. Obviously the Speedway Control Board thought otherwise because they called both Mike and myself to a special hearing early in October, 1968, to see if we could sort out our differences.

The fact that I was allowed to leave Newcastle a few months later proves, I believe, that the Board fully realised that it was impossible for us to settle our differences amicably.

Even that wasn't the final instalment in our season of bickering. It carried right until the end of the British League season.

I continued to ride out the 1968 season and probably the worst move – as far as I was concerned – came when I lined up for my final two meetings.

Before the meetings I had sent my bikes to New Zealand where I was to spend the winter and one of the clauses in my contract says that a rider is responsible for supplying a machine in good working condition for his own use.

For the match at Wimbledon on Thursday, 24th October I had arranged to borrow a bike from Ken Vale, one of my best friends in the sport. Ken had been very kind to me during my early days at Wimbledon, we had remained friends since and he agreed to loan me his bike.

I rode Ken's in the first race and if I remember correctly dropped a point to Olle Nygren. On getting back to the pits I discovered a crack in Ken's frame and finished the meeting riding three different bikes. Even so I was Newcastle's top scorer with 10 points.

The following night we were at Wolverhampton and again I had arranged to borrow a friend's machine – this time belonging to Pete Jarman.

While all the riders were warming up their machines before the meeting was due to start Pete was warming up his machine for me to ride. I was just standing around when Mike came into the pits and asked to know where my bike was.

I told him MY bike was not there but I had a bike to ride. It seemed to me that this was another matter on which we were not going to be able to agree, and our subsequent conversation appeared to confirm that impression.

I was at the end of my tether and ready to go and began getting changed about ten minutes before the tapes were due to go up. Pete Jarman came into the dressing room and managed to talk me into going out to ride in the meeting by saying it would be very bad for me if I didn't and that as I had put up with everything for so long I should ride just that one last meeting.

He persuaded me to see sense and riding his bike I dropped two points in my first race but finished with three wins on the trot and once again topped the Diamonds score-chart with ten points.

I left England the next day to race in America and as far as I was concerned if I didn't get a transfer that was the last meeting I would ever ride in England.

But I later learned of complaints that I had failed to supply my own bike for these last two meetings – even though I was top scorer for my side on both occasions!

I think it was probably this incident which convinced the Speedway Control Board that Mike Parker and I would never be able to get on as long as we were connected with the same track.

Since that day at Wolverhampton I have never spoken to Mike Parker. He has spoken to me once – when he was introducing the riders at the British League Riders Final at Belle Vue when he told me: 'Step forward' during the presentation. Other than that we have completely ignored each other and any conversation about riding for his Wolverhampton track has been done through his business partner, Bill Bridgett, with whom I have had no argument.

It might be of interest to tell you a little bit about what went on at that Speedway Control Board meeting we were both asked to attend.

It was suggested that I wanted to leave Newcastle for these three reasons.

(1) I didn't like the track.

(2) I wanted to ride more in Europe on a Sunday and being with a Monday track stopped me.

(3) Other promoters had made bigger under-the-counter offers than Newcastle could afford.

When the Chairman of the Control Board, Mr Nelson Mills-Baldwin asked for my answers I told him:

(1) As I held the track record and had only been beaten a handful of times at Newcastle in two or three seasons I could hardly argue I didn't like the track. Although I did call it a scrambles/cum-trials track I was happy to ride the track because personally I never worried about a track's condition.

(2) No matter where I rode in Europe, even behind the Iron Curtain, I could still get back to Newcastle in time for a Monday meeting.

(3) I told him that if Mike Parker gave me every penny he had it would still not be enough to buy me for another season and that it was NOT just a question of money.

Possibly – almost certainly – I was to blame for a number of our arguments. I accept this and realise that basically we just couldn't get on. Of course money came into it but as far as I was concerned this wasn't the sole reason I wanted to leave Mike Parker's track. And it was obvious the Control Board understood the situation as I was told I wouldn't be at Newcastle in 1969!

While our arguments had been raging I had had offers from all but four of the country's promoters asking me to ride for them in 1969.

Even when I went back to New Zealand I received several calls a week from Britain trying to tempt me back to ride in various colours.

And in no case was a promoter foolish enough to suggest that I joined his track for the agreed pay rates!

The next I heard about a move was a telegram from the Promoters' Association saying I had been allocated to Hackney Wick. By this time I had decided I wanted to ride for Belle Vue and because I had waited so long for a move I thought I could afford to stay in New Zealand until I got the track I wanted.

I have nothing personal against Hackney Wick or its promoter Len Silver but I felt that I would be much happier in Manchester than based in London.

One of the main reasons was that I had lived in Manchester since I came back to Britain in 1963 and my children were all used to going to school in Manchester. I felt to uproot them and set up a new home in London would not be to their advantage.

Manchester was also extremely convenient for my continental trips and being a Saturday night track it meant that it was generally fairly easy to catch an early Sunday morning flight to the continent.

I must stress that my decision was not based on the sort of contract that I was offered.

Since 1963 I had always asked to be paid what are considered 'illegal' prizes. What I would ask for was a set guaranteed amount of prize money for any open meeting that I competed in.

By the time I was European champion in 1966 I was asking and receiving from most promoters guarantees for open meetings. In league matches, of course, I rode for normal start and points money as well as in any other official meeting.

It was purely in those meetings where I was being booked as an attraction that I asked for a guarantee which could be paid no matter how many points I scored.

While these are 'illegal' payments I believe I have a human right to ask – while the promoter has a human right to say no.

As a shopkeeper can put his own price on his own goods so I believe can a speedway rider. It is up to the customer (or promoter) to decide whether or not the goods are worth the money.

For a long time these payments were kept secret and known only to those closely connected with the sport and, certainly not to the people on the terraces.

However once or twice it has come out into the open. On one

occasion, for example, the Exeter management made it public via their programme that I wasn't riding in a meeting because I had asked for a guarantee.

This was, though, an isolated incident and generally the promoters were happy to give me the cash. After I won my third World title I decided to make the guarantee aspect of speedway public and I then began to ask for a £100 guarantee before I would ride in any open meeting.

Another storm blew up when I refused to attend the Wimbledon 'Laurels' meeting because the promoter wouldn't meet my demands. I was eventually reported to the Board for failing to appear in the meeting but they dismissed the charge.

According to the rules, as a World Champion I am legally entitled to an extra £10 for any open meeting in which I compete. Is that really all a World Champion should be worth?

I certainly don't think so. Without the hefty guarantees I would have to think about leaving British speedway. After all, I can fly to Germany for a Sunday afternoon meeting and earn £300 or £400 for a couple of races. It would be more profitable to do this than ride in three open meetings in England under the legal payment system.

While all this is, according to the rule-book, illegal it goes on with the knowledge, if not blessing, of most of the promoters.

One further point: when I captained Great Britain in an official test tour of Sweden in 1970 I asked for and got a handsome fee for the tour regardless of how may times I rode and how well I scored. In other words I got a guarantee for an international tour!

Illegal payments are so rife in speedway – I know of riders who have been given a house to sign a three or five year contract with a club – that it would be impossible to stop it.

That's why I feel the full extent to which it goes on should be made public. Certainly I consider that it is a proper right of a rider – no matter who he is – to be able to negotiate something 'on the side'.

After all surely a man who is a drawcard is worth more money than someone else who may be purely filling a spot in the programme.

Some people may say that by being given a guarantee for a meeting I would not try to my utmost. Take the Swedish tour for example. I scored a maximum in the first test match, was Britain's top scorer overall and skippered the tourists to a test win against a country recognised as probably the finest in speedway.

And if there is still any doubt you only have to look back at my record of individual meetings during the past seven years to see that I always gave my 100 per cent while I was being 'illegally' paid.

13

The Man I Hated . . .

Speedway is a dangerous sport. Probably one of the most dangerous in the world and certainly a pastime that would prove too demanding for the weak or faint-hearted.

Injury is never very far away and so much depends on trust between the riders. Trust. Trust that the rider you are against will do nothing deliberate to try and injure you.

Ninety-nine times out of a hundred that trust is there. But always there is the exception and there have been quite a few private feuds between riders. The sort of feud that is never known to the fan. The sort of feud that can be dangerous and can end in trouble at the best – and death at the worst!

That is the sort of feud that I never dreamt I would get involved in. But I did.

The rider I was involved with was one of the top boys in the Provincial League until I came on the scene. If it had been possible I'm sure that the folk from his track-town would have given him the keys to the city! His style was rightly familiar at the Provincial League tracks.

I chatted with him quite a lot during 1963 and the early part of 1964. I genuinely thought that we were at least colleagues if not warm personal friends.

And I certainly trusted him then. Until one night fairly early in the '64 season. It was a match between my club Newcastle and his club.

When we met for the first time that Monday night he gated slightly ahead of me from the inside position. As I attempted to go past him on the outside on the first turn – I knew that there would be no room between him and the white line but that there would be plenty of room on the outside – he seemed to make straight for the fence in the middle of the corner, with me trapped outside him.

I sensed straight away that something was wrong. In the split second I had to make up my mind what to do, I flicked my back wheel round in an attempt to slow down. It was the only way I knew of avoiding one of two things – a head on collision with my opponent or a head on collision with the fence.

We had both slowed down considerably to barely walking pace, so by this time the other two riders had picked up grip and gone tearing down the back straight. My opponent, as the man dictating terms, knew exactly what he was doing and corrected his course within a foot of the fence to come out of the turn in control of his bike.

By the time I'd sorted myself out I'd given him quite a start and I'm sure he realised that I was after him. We both passed the other two riders as if they weren't on the track and I managed to make up ground. Going into each turn I was only a foot or so away from him.

In my own mind I was determined to hit him if I could. But I was just that little bit short of being able to hit him midships and I knew that if I hit his back wheel I would have gone over.

I was so angry that I didn't care if I went – as long as he went with me. I would have willingly gone through the fence with him just to make sure he was there.

Try as I might I couldn't make up that vital foot or so. Being angry I probably made mistakes that I wouldn't have made had I kept a cool head.

I tried to get him every corner instead of collecting my thoughts and planning how I would pass him as I would have done had it been an ordinary race.

Eventually we both completed four laps and as I followed him into the pits I was still completely mystified as to what had caused the incident on the first turn.

Back in the pits I demanded an explanation and his only answer was, 'you've got a short memory, Mauger; you've done it twice to me this season already.'

I couldn't remember any previous incidents between the pair of us and even to this day I can't recall when – or if – it had happened, as he has never been any more specific.

At the time I was holding the league's individual match-race championship and was due to defend it against his team's highest scorer. This looked as if it would be our friend and I'm sure the crowd were on their toes expecting fireworks when we met in the first race after the interval.

But I'd studied the programme and worked out that we should both qualify for the last race of the evening.

I figured that he could wait . . . and I'd momentarily shelve all ideas of taking him into the fence until I'd made sure of winning the big event of the evening.

I'm sure that he must have failed to read my thoughts – for he never really challenged me seriously in that particular race. Certainly something was lacking in his challenge for he would normally have given me one of my toughest races. Instead I led comfortably from start to finish.

I was right in my reading of the programme. We both qualified for the final race.

The draw for starting positions couldn't have been better. I was drawn one (on the inside), he was drawn two; Mike Watkin on position three; and Bill Andrew on gate four.

Before we even left the pits I had had a quiet word with my two team-mates and warned them to stay out of the way as I was determined to teach our opponent a lesson.

I deliberately let him gate slightly ahead of me and we stayed in that position for the fifty odd yards to the beginning of the first turn. As we went into the turn I accelerated and with our elbows locked we rode straight towards the fence.

As he had done in our first meeting I was able to pull round short of the fence to save hitting it myself. He could have got out of it by taking the coward's way out and shutting off. Instead he chose to duel with me right up to the fence and in a funny sort of way I respected him for it.

As I went down the back straight I saw the red light come on telling everyone the race had been stopped. I immediately thought that the referee was stopping the race so that he could exclude me for dangerous riding.

It wasn't until I had cruised back to the pits quarter that I saw my Newcastle team-mate Bill Andrew in a heap with our opponent in the fence. It was obvious that Bill hadn't taken too much notice of my warning.

Fortunately Bill got up okay – but his bike was in a sorry state having hit one of the lighting stanchions. However, Mike Parker helped him towards the cost of repairing it and Bill was quite happy at the eventual outcome.

My opponent, however, couldn't have been so happy. He gashed his foot and subsequently was out for four or five weeks.

As far as I was concerned that was the end of the incident. We'd had one go at each other and while I had come off best from our two clashes I thought everything would be forgotten.

A couple of weeks later I heard that he was putting it around in the Midlands that I wouldn't be around to defend my Provincial League Riders Championship.

I didn't take too much notice of it because I thought that it was probably a few scandal-mongers trying to work up a real hatred between the pair of us.

Personally I don't think I would have done anything about it had I not got my own back that night. There was a lot of difference between holding a grudge for one evening – and retaining it for what might have been several weeks. What happened at Newcastle came about because I was in a temper and not because I coldly set out to injure another rider.

Our clash at Newcastle had been in June and a month later I was due to ride at my opponent's home track in a special trophy event.

There had been quite a lot of talk there about what would happen to me when I went down for the meeting. So much so that Mike Parker made a phone call to the management threatening to take action if anything happened to me while I was at their track.

By the time the meeting came around my 'friend' was ready to begin riding again, even though many people thought he was rushing his comeback.

I was only in the dressing room five minutes when I found that he was, in fact, still angry with me. The dressing room was partitioned off into two separate rooms – one for home riders, the other for the visitors.

He came into the visitors' section making all sorts of threats. I wasn't standing for that. After a few minutes shouting and arguing at each other we both lost our tempers and ended up fighting in the middle of the dressing room.

The rest of the boys broke us up before either of us caused too much damage.

Everyone expected there to be trouble on the track when we met – but it never got that far. In his first ride he was leading as he went into a bend. It had been raining and the track was greasy. He came out of the bend, and lost control on a greasy patch and went down in the path of Jack Kitchen who was following closely behind. Jack whipped his bike down but couldn't avoid the fallen rider. 'Kitch' went over him – and he was carted off to hospital. So our clash hadn't come off and I was pleased to drive away from the track in one piece – and with the Trophy previously held by you know who!

We were to meet again several times during the latter half of the season, with him continually threatening to put me out of the Provincial League Riders' Final and me continually managing to stay out of his way so that he couldn't do it.

However, when the championship was over and the title in my pocket again, I was ready for the show-down.

Before going out for the presentation at Belle Vue I looked around for him and eventually found him in the shower room. I told him: 'I've bloody well tolerated you long enough. Now I've won the championship again I'm ready for you. So any time you're willing, I am.'

I don't know whether this scared him or whether he, too, was completely fed up with the feud.

But whatever it was, I raced against him often in the following season and we never had any problems. That's not to say we became firm friends . . . we have just kept fairly well apart.

He is the one and only opponent I have ever tried to mix it with in this way. Since then I've had one or two argy-bargies with various other riders but it has always been nothing more than an honest-to-goodness clash where neither of us have been willing to give ground.

Many people may think I still hold a grudge against Sweden's Bernie Persson following our battle in the 1967 World Final at Wembley.

But as far as I'm concerned that was an isolated incident that happened during a meeting and although I believe it cost me the World Final I accepted it as part of racing. As I have said in an earlier chapter, on World Final night you can't expect to meet 15 riders willing to let you do what you want.

The only other incident that caused anything like the furore surrounding the affair just described came in the 1969 International event at Wimbledon.

Trevor Hedge and I had tied with 13 points and needed a run-off to decide who won the new £350 Jap and the Loughborough Trophy.

During the run-off we swapped the lead several times in the early stages of the race.

Going into the pits bend on the third lap Hedgey was inside me as we went into the turn and neither of us was willing to give an inch.

As I was on the outside and the track extremely slick, there simply wasn't enough shale to hold me up going into the corner at such a pace and I fell. In circumstances like this the rider on the outside is always first to go.

There was quite an uproar from the crowd as I went down and Hedgey carried on riding the last two laps on his own. He had to thread his way carefully through the seemingly scores of track officials who had dashed across to try and help me.

The referee, acting quite correctly according to the rule book, allowed the race to go on as the fans screamed for a re-run.

No doubt my supporters were shouting that Hedgey should be excluded for pushing me off . . . and no doubt his fans were lapping up the sight of seeing me spreadeagled across the track.

Once I had picked myself up I dashed to the phone on the centre green opposite the judges' box to protest to the referee.

It was not that I honestly thought that Hedgey had treated me unfairly but because I thought that in view of the closeness of the racing the referee might order a re-run. As a professional I consider I would have been foolish not to have complained when there was an outside chance that the referee might have seen my point of view and given me another chance against Hedgey.

Once it was obvious the referee was sticking to his decision I went straight into the pits and into the dressing room to change. It wasn't until I was in the shower that a Wimbledon official told me I was needed for the presentation.

By then I was hardly dressed for the occasion and had no qualms about telling the official that I wasn't going to parade in front of 20,000 fans wearing nothing more than a bath-robe!

Unfortunately many of the fans took my non-appearance at the presentation as a slight against the referee and, more particularly, against Hedgey.

In fact nothing could have been further from the truth. At no time previous to the run-off had I been told that the runner-up would be needed for any presentation.

And as far as the pits bend incident with Hedgey was concerned I in no way blamed him for what had happened. Like any other rider he had refused to 'chicken out' going into a bend and he was the one who came out winner.

There's certainly been no acrimony between us since and I never ever considered trying to get my revenge.

For there was nothing there in the beginning. . . .

14

The Fall — and Fall — of the British Lion

In recent times England has provided a World Champion in practically every sport. But not speedway. . . .

Since 1950 only one Englishman has won a World Speedway Championship final.

That was Liverpudlian Peter Craven who took the crown in both 1955 and 1962.

And to make the English story even more depressing, apart from Craven no Englishman has ever looked like winning the title! In fact the last Englishman other than Craven to stand on the first three dais was Arthur Forrest way back in 1956.

Look back through the years from the day the World Championship was launched in its present form and there are few English names gracing the championship story.

Tommy Price was champion in 1949; Welshman Freddie Williams in 1950 and 1953; and Craven.

Three champions in more than twenty years! What a sad condemnation for the country that is to all intents and purposes the home of speedway.

Take the last ten years. In the last decade the late Peter Craven is the only English-born rider to finish in the first three. In fact stretching the decade to 15 years Forrest is the only man other than Craven to have the famed tractor ride as third-place man.

In the same fifteen years my own hometown of Christchurch has provided TWO champions. And another who had made the town his own.

Which brings me to the question . . . WHY?

The question that every speedway supporter in the world is asking. Why can't an Englishman hold his head high in the company of the world's best.

To sum it up in one short, sharp word: PROFESSIONALISM.

Or rather the lack of it. Since I've been in Britain I've seen a number of riders who would be capable of lifting the crown. They have the talent . . . the potential . . . and what's more the opportunities.

Unlike the Australasian riders who come over to make their name and their living in British speedway the home-based riders do not have the problems or the worries of travelling thousands of miles to ride regularly.

It is all on the doorstep of the English boy. His nearest track must be less than an hour's car drive away. The opportunity is there alright.

But that is not enough. To win a World title needs more than talent, ability and opportunity. It needs dedication.

Which is where the English rider has fallen down. I am not saying it is impossible for an English rider to win the World Championship. What I am saying is why one has not done it in the last ten years.

I've already mentioned that they lack professionalism. Just what does this word mean? To me it really means dedication.

To win a World final you have to be dedicated. You have to give up some of the pleasures of life. This means you give up absolutely everything in your quest. You must want it badly enough to give up everything.

Socially you become a hermit. There's no late night dancing. No through-till-early-morning drinking. No womanising.

You must have only one thought on your mind . . . how you are going to beat the rest of the world. And you must be prepared to work to that end.

I know of English finalists who have gone out on the town the night before the big event!

And you must go into that meeting convinced that you are capable of winning. Not like one English rider who came up to me before a recent final and said: 'I'm amazed that I've got this far. I haven't got a chance so I shall only be going for a ride.'

And that was a young man who had already proved himself among the world's top sixteen. That was negative thinking if I ever heard it.

While this is the most blatant example of a lack of faith in one's own ability it is somewhat symptomatic of a lot of the English riders who get to the final.

There are, of course, exceptions. Some of the local boys have great faith in their own capabilities. What they lack is something other than confidence.

A speedway rider is an athlete. And like any athlete he must build up to a peak. It is no good reaching that peak seven days before a World final. And equally it is no good scaling the peak seven days after the final.

The peak and the final must coincide. Often I've seen an English boy break track record after track record in the fortnight before the final.

Or alternatively they've come back from the final and gone like a bomb at every track they have visited. Sometimes they've beaten me and the fans have liked it.

But they've also wondered why I hadn't been beaten in the final. What they rarely seem to understand is that I've geared my whole life to being at the top of my form when it really mattered.

I don't want to go down as the man who broke the track record at Poole. Track records mean very little in comparison to winning a world title.

Several times in recent years Nigel Boocock, probably the best Englishman since Peter Craven, has discussed the use of nitromethane (a powerful additive for racing fuels used in drag racing) in his column in the national weekly *Motor Cycle News*.

Without exception he has condemned its use, claiming that it is expensive, hard to attain, harmful to the engine and above all provides its user with an unfair advantage.

Nigel is and always has been a very good friend of mine and I have a great admiration for his ability, determination and forthrightness.

But Nigel, my old mate, you are falling for a widely held and popular misconception.

Back in the fifties they said it was the special cam shaft that won Barry Briggs his titles. Later they said it was nitro that won me my titles.

Nothing could be further from the truth. Because Barry and I won our titles on standard equipment. But I can't deny that the experience we had both gained from using the 'extras' helped us on final night.

From my knowledge of the late fifties Barry was using special cam shafts in the Jap engine a couple of years before any English boys latched onto the idea.

Similarly I used nitro-methane – now banned at international meetings – two or three seasons before the English boys even talked about it. Had an English rider bothered to find out they, too, would have been able to use a special cam-shaft or nitro-methane. But they didn't. Instead they seemed content to amble on in the same old steady way.

I used it for one reason . . . because I THOUGHT it would help me. And I considered it was worth the cost – no matter what – worth the trouble of obtaining it – no matter what – and worth the risk of harming my engine – no matter what. IF in the end it proved to be of benefit to me.

Nitro-methane is highly volatile and if used incorrectly it can harm an engine. In fact it can wreck one.

But it was by using it that I learnt when I could use it and, more important, when I shouldn't use it. It was this knowledge I gained while experimenting that taught me not to use it in a World final.

As Nigel says it can harm an engine, and one must finish five races to be in with any sort of chance of winning a World final.

During the 1970 season I could have named a dozen British League riders who used nitro-methane at one time or another. And not one of them was an Englishman! !

At the same time two or three came up to me at odd times to talk about it. They asked me how often I used it; what quantities I used; which tracks I used it at; what atmospheric conditions were needed to use it; and where could they buy it.

I could tell from their conversation that they wanted to try it but something was holding them back.

I wonder – was it because it was too expensive? Was it because it was too hard to obtain? Or was it because they thought it would harm their engines?

None of them seemed to have either the courage, or the professionalism, to find out!

The twelve 'foreigners' experimenting with it didn't seem to worry about any of these drawbacks.

Was it mere coincidence that of the twelve 'foreigners' six of us got through to the World Final in Poland? Of that six at least three of us had learnt enough during the season *NOT* to use it at the World final under the prevailing conditions.

I don't believe that it was by chance that half of the riders who took pains to experiment during the season reached the World final.

It is more likely that it is just another example of what professionalism is all about.

Let's look at another facet of this game. Last year the World Final was held behind the Iron Curtain for the first time in the dreaded hunting ground of all British riders . . . Poland.

In the past, touring sides had been to the Soviet sphere and come away soundly beaten. I'd been in the teams myself and knew what it was like to be on the losing side.

Once it was revealed that the meeting would be at Wroclaw half of the English boys gave up the ghost straight away. They were demoralised.

Even in the early qualifying rounds they thought they were fighting a losing battle. What does it matter if we get through they thought. If we don't get thrashed at Leningrad in the European Final, we'll get a hiding when we get to Poland.

One by one the top English names were toppled. Sensationally some went out in the qualifying rounds. Others fell by the wayside in the British Final.

Come the Nordic/British Final and there were only three left – Roy Trigg, Arnold Haley and Trevor Hedge. Only one – Hedge – got through to the Russian-staged European Final.

It was as England's sole representative that he went to the World Final – even though he was leaving back home a good handful of riders with better records in international competition.

What happened to the rest? Many were, I am convinced, beaten by the thought of that track in Wroclaw!

It is not, however, a criticism that can be levelled solely at the riders. Too many of their promoters adopted a defeatist attitude before the qualifying rounds were over.

Instead of boosting the morale and stock of the English riders they were putting them down. A week before the European final one senior administrator turned round to me and said: 'Let's hope you and your two Kiwi mates – meaning Barry Briggs and Ronnie Moore – get through to the final. Otherwise I can't see Britain being represented in Poland.'

He obviously didn't have any faith in Trevor – so how could Trevor believe in his own ability?

But there was an even more blatant example of what a promoter shouldn't do. There was still a sting in the tail.

Two days before the final the British-based party was staying in the Grand Hotel in Wroclaw. A senior promoter was in the same hotel. He seemed to think that only Barry or myself had any chance of finishing in the first three.

We were sitting in a group chatting away when he lolled back in his chair, rolled his head, and simply drawled: 'We – ell . . . Hedgey would have been better off if he'd have stayed at home and ridden in the Southern Riders' Championship!'

I'm not going to name these two promoters but rest assured they are among those who are considered the most senior in British speedway through age, experience, and service to the sport.

In this the sort of example they should set? I know that Hedgey was aware of their feelings. It can't have given him any encouragement in the final.

On scanning the list of finalists I certainly had more faith in Hedgey than either of these two promoters did.

And but for a succession of mishaps he could well have finished high up in the final reckoning.

But it is this sort of thing that is holding the English rider back. To win a World final you need the confidence and encouragement that is so vital. Without it you are lost.

Today I consider that I could name three or four of the new wave of English riders who could, in future years, become world champions.

All it needs is for them to learn the one basic ingredient that separates a world-class rider from a World Champion.

And that ingredient is . . . professionalism!

15

Speedway Stateside — The Truth about America

Before and after the last war speedway held a vice-like grip on the American public.

Scores of tracks sprang up throughout the States and many of their top riders visited Britain determined to emulate Jack and Cordy Milne who had dominated the World Speedway Championship.

But during the fifties speedway all but died across the Atlantic and it wasn't until three or four seasons ago that we saw signs of a revival.

I had read a little about new tracks opening in the States but didn't know a lot about it until I got a phone call during the summer of 1967 asking if I would go across to the States to ride at a series of meetings in California the following year.

So straight after Newcastle's last league meeting of the season at Wolverhampton I dashed down to Heathrow Airport for my first trip to America.

As so often happens the plane was late and by the time we touched down at Los Angeles Airport I was already late for the meeting. Old time star Pee Wee Cullum – once a circus clown who became one of America's top speedway riders after the war – was at the airport to meet me and I was whisked off to the 210-yard Whiteman track, about twenty miles from the airport.

I thought I had gone to the wrong place! It wasn't like anything that I had known as speedway. The riders were on outdated, ancient machines. Their bars were dropped low down like in pre-war leg-trailing times and they were just riding round. There was no semblance of a slide and it was apparent that they had little idea of genuine speedway.

I think the only new machine they had was for me and I seized that in practice but they wheeled out another bike for me and I won my first five races and smashed the one, two and four lap records. It wasn't that I was going so fast it was just that the standard was incredibly low. I didn't know whether to laugh – or cry.

Soon, however, things improved. I ran a couple of training schools and the first thing I did was to move the handlebars, and get the Yanks to let a little bit of air out of their tyres.

With their low bars and hard tyres it would have been impossible for them to turn quickly and once I had explained the basic rudiments of speedway in the sixties-style they began to improve.

One thing I soon realised was that all the Yanks were eager to learn and would not only listen to what I was telling them but would try and put it into operation out on the track.

Within a fortnight the standard had improved noticeably and the race times of the locals came spiralling down. They were still a long way short of a British League level but when I left Los Angeles I knew that the Americans were going the right way.

A few days after I had arrived in the States Barry Briggs jetted in and between us I think we taught the local boys quite a lot about speedway. Certainly they seemed to take notice of everything we told them and it was heartening to see the television and newspaper interest that our visits aroused.

Encouraged by our visit Yanks Rick Woods, Chuck Jones and DeWayne Keeter travelled on to Australia during the winter months and shocked the tough Aussie crowds by their incredible progress in such a short time.

Chuck, unfortunately, was later involved in an accident on the Aussie bowl that ended his speedway career, and was confined to a wheelchair as a result of spinal injuries sustained in the crash. Now he is able to walk on crutches.

DeWayne accepted an offer from English promoter to join British League Division One side Leicester for the entire 1969 season and although he failed to reach heat leader status he showed enough skill, ability and tenacity to become an extremely valuable member of the side. After failing to score in his first few meetings – and looking, frankly, out of his depth he improved tremendously and by the end of the year was capable of picking up the occasional double-figure score.

DeWayne, though wasn't retained for the 1970 season and since then he has transferred his allegiance to the financially more worthwhile Class 'C' grade of American racing – a form of motor-cycle sport that I shall discuss in considerable detail later in this chapter.

Throughout 1969 the Americans ran a complete season of speedway – the season running parallel to the British season – and in late October I returned to California for another season under the American banner.

By then the Whiteman track had closed down but had been replaced by a smaller circuit at Costa Mesa. All the Americans competed regularly at the 190-yard track which certainly ranked as the smallest speedway track in operation in the World.

The tightness of the circuit certainly caught me out – and Briggo also. After over-doing it on a couple of occasions in the heats I came off in the final and sustained concussion. Luckily a few days later I had recovered and felt nothing more than a headache. Briggo also took a trip to the doctors and finished with a broken toe after a particularly spectacular fall.

Two other British based riders also joined us on this trip – Australian champion Jim Airey and volatile Scotsman Bert Harkins – and they too had their fair share of thrills and spills as they tried to adjust to a track that was no bigger than a cycle-speedway raceway.

While Costa Mesa was the established senior American track we also had a trip out into the country to try and raise funds for a school swimming pool at Santa Barbara. We used the school's quarter mile running track so we British boys felt more at home and cleaned up in a big way.

Mr Harry Oxley, promoter at Costa Mesa, was delighted with our return trip and the main point that struck me on my second trip was the steady improvement in the American riders.

Equipment had improved 100 per cent with nearly all the top-liners mounted on new, or nearly new, Jap or Jawa machines. Steve Bast, who was later to join Wembley for an ill-fated month, had overtaken Rick Woods as top Yank and added the American National Speedway Championship to his Californian title.

Woods was still close at hand with old timers Stu Morley and Don Hawley – a tourist with the American side that visited Britain in the fifties – using their experience to good advantage.

I felt that before the Americans were to make real progress in speedway there was a need for more than one track at Costa Mesa. Its very shape and length would prove more of a handicap than anything else to any American wanting to try his luck in Britain.

And so it proved many months later when teenager Steve Bast –

one of three racing Basts, his younger brother Mike and his uncle Harlan being the others – accepted an offer to join Wembley Lions as replacement for the five times World Champion Ove Fundin.

Bast scored a few points for the Lions but found it difficult to adjust to the larger British tracks and after less than a month decided to call it a day and shot back to America in time to lose his national title to the fiery Woods.

I still feel that had Bast joined the Lions at the beginning of the season and had he been willing to give himself a few months to adjust to the tougher school of racing he would have been a top man in a very short time.

Rain – the old enemy in Britain – also decimated my second American trip because it meant I had to call off plans to run another series of training schools.

Incidentally an unusual point that was raised when it started raining was the universal acceptance by American riders, promoters and fans that there would be no meeting in the wet. A far cry from England when some promoters think we can ride in a hailstorm!

Much of the American way of life could be recommended. The riders, for example, were all sponsored by local businessmen and very few of them had any financial worries about providing themselves with a machine and leathers.

Perhaps this has been the main reason there hasn't been an influx of Yanks willing to try their luck in Britain. Financially they are far better off staying in their own country.

It was during this 1969 trip that I was approached by a representative of the Japanese Kawasaki motor-cycle firm asking if I would compete on Class 'C' during the early part of 1970. Twelve months previous Barry Briggs had done so with another organisation and I was keen to give it a try.

My first excursion into Class 'C' was something of a hurried venture. Kawasaki sent me a couple of 250 c.c. engines from America and I had a frame made in London by Alf Hagon.

Neither Alf nor I knew what we really had to make for this type of racing and when I got over to America it was hardly what I had expected. The first meeting was to be at the massive Houston Astrodome with further meetings at Daytona, Florida.

It is hard to explain what Class 'C' is other than it is a combination of most motor-cycle sports with hardly any real relationship with speedway.

The bikes are specially tuned road bikes, something of a cross between a powerful road racer and a scrambles machine. The circuits are a lot bigger than a normal American speedway track and all the machines are fitted with gears and brakes. There is no sliding around a corner at all and you ride as if you were at the Isle of Man.

Unlike speedway there is no set programme and as many riders as want can take part in the meeting. When I arrived at Houston I found I was just one of 170 blokes wanting to take part.

Anyone can put in an entry and all the entries are accepted. It is a procedure that has its good and its bad points. The good things are that everyone gets a chance of racing in the actual championship. What usually happens is that everyone who has entered has to undergo a time trial and the fastest 36 or 48 go through into the final.

On the other hand I really think it reduces the standard of racing because the top boys who could get better only have a couple of practice laps – otherwise the 170 would never be whittled down to a reasonable number.

Because of bad weather I never had a chance to test the bike in England and I hadn't ridden it at all until I came to my time-trial. The Americans use a Pirelli rear tyre or a Dunlop K70 which is very similar to a road racing tyre – completely the opposite to a conventional speedway tyre. I went there with a Barum back tyre as I would use on a speedway bike. The track was a little bit bumpy in practice and it had quite a bit of loose dirt on it and I was well pleased with the way I went.

After practice I came to the time trials. I was warned that I had only two laps to go and they took the fastest of those two laps as the time to count. Before I went out Kawasaki told me not to be too disappointed if I didn't get through but I think I surprised them by putting up a fairly good time and that left me comfortably within the qualifying limits.

The track was still a bit bumpy and there was still a bit of dirt on it so I was satisfied that the Barum tyre was suitable for the final even though Briggo and I were the only two qualifiers using it.

That night I was to get quite a shock. Between the time trials and that actual meeting the track was graded really smooth, and had been watered and tyre-packed so that it was just hard and smooth like a linoleum floor without an ounce of grip on it.

Briggo, wisely, had changed to a Pirelli but partly through

ignorance of racing on that surface and partly because of being pleased with my practice I decided to stick to the Barum. The 48 finalists were split into four heats with 12 riders per heat, the top six going into two semi-finals.

I learnt a whole lot in the first five yards of my first race! I let the clutch out and thought the chain had come off! The bike never even moved . . . the tyre just wasn't getting any grip at all.

Eventually I coaxed it into the first turn quite a way behind the other eleven riders . . . and that's the way I stayed for all six laps gradually dropping further and further behind.

I probably looked good because I was sideways all the way but I wasn't going very fast and when I looked back at it a few weeks later I accepted that this was bound to happen because of it having been such a hurriedly put together project.

I am positive that if the track had been in the same condition for the final as for the time trial and practice I would have gone very well. But my lack of knowledge of the technicalities of Class 'C' racing brought its expected reward!

Other than the wrong choice of tyre I also felt that the head angle of my frame had been too steep. From the Houston meeting I went back to Australia for a few weeks before returning to the States for a further catalogue of Class 'C' racing.

I was due in America for the Daytona Speedway week – the biggest date in the world's motor-cycling calendar. The speed week lasts from Monday through to Sunday and I was to ride in two short-track Class 'C' meetings.

Throughout the week there are speed trials, road racing, enduros (endurance races), moto-cross, the Daytona 200 mile road race and every form of racing you can think of. My own particular events were on the Friday and Saturday nights and it was impossible to get any practice before the Friday afternoon about an hour before the meeting.

There were so many riders waiting to have practice that I went to the line on Friday night for the first heat having had only two laps practice.

Although I would have changed to the Pirelli tyre after my experience at Houston the Daytona track appeared to be more like a speedway track surface and I kept to the Barum tyres. Again I had made a mistake and didn't go so well.

There weren't so many competitors on the Saturday night and

I managed to get in about three short practice sessions, a couple of laps each. This time I put a Pirelli tyre on and it made such a difference that it was well nigh unbelievable. It was as if I was riding another bike.

Everything built up to a final of 48 riders and in the qualifying races I turned in the second fastest time of the meeting. It meant that I had the pole position as fastest qualifier in my semi-final but I made a bad start and never really recovered.

When the Americans go into the corner they knock the throttle off and a lot of them pull a decompression lifter which on a two-stroke operates as an air-brake and slows down which is the opposite to what I would do on a speedway track.

I found myself running into the back of slower competitors on the bends and a couple of times I got up to fourth position and among the qualifiers for the next stage but I would keep hitting a rider in front and while I was sorting myself out on the gears others passed me and I eventually finished about sixth in my heat.

However I learned a lot during the trip and I know that in future I will be able to do better. The Kawasaki engine I rode was only 238 c.c. and a standard model whereas I was racing against full 250 c.c. bikes and although my engine was very good in itself it wasn't made for the Class 'C' racing and wasn't quite strong enough.

While I don't think that I could ever be as keen to ride on Class 'C' as I am on speedway there is a great deal of money in this form of racing in America . . . far more than there is in English speedway.

However I earn a considerable amount of money racing in Europe every Sunday – usually it runs into nearly five figures over the season – and I would have to consider this carefully before I ever decided to make America my permanent home.

I still get a great deal of pleasure out of riding speedway and so far I get a lot more pleasure out of that than the Class 'C' racing which lacks a lot of speedway's excitement.

During 1970 I had to think very carefully as to whether I should retire from active British League speedway to spend more time in America but after weighing up all the pros and cons for several weeks I decided to stay in Britain.

Financially I lost money by doing so – but the fact that I would have had to live in the States affected my decision greatly. While I have always enjoyed a month's trip to America I do not feel that I could happily uproot my family and live in California.

Education played a great part in my decision because I still believe that England provides my children with the finest schooling in the world.

I felt far happier at the prospect of Julie, Kym and Debbie going to school in Cheshire than I would have done if I had to look for a school for them in Los Angeles or a neighbouring community.

America, though, is a new horizon and I am sure that as the months go by so the lure and pull of America will get stronger and stronger. Had there been a really active speedway scene in California it may have altered my mind. But as yet American speedway is still in its infancy although it is growing steadily with each passing season.

The American progress has not been entirely without its setbacks because wealthy businessman Pete Palmer, who finances the successful Great Bear Racing Team in the States, opened at a couple of new centres during 1970 and had to close down within a few short weeks because of lack of public response.

It was hoped that there would be six tracks operating on a weekly programme basis in the States during '70 – at Cornel Corners, San Fernando (at one time a flourishing Class 'C' centre); San Diego, Bakersfield, Lancaster and, of course, Costa Mesa.

Lancaster Park – with Pete Palmer holding the reigns – opened early in the year but despite a small fortune being spent on the track it had to shut down after only a handful of meetings with an average attendance of under the 500 mark!

Famous race-car driver Dr Lou Sell became interested and announced his plans to bring speedway to another Los Angeles township – Bakersfield. He did in fact achieve what he set out to do and had a fairly promising season.

Meanwhile in Britain a lot of so-called experts began to write up the American story as if the Yanks were on the verge of becoming World beaters. There was talk of an American side coming to tour Britain's Second Division tracks but this never got off the ground.

Steve Bast did come though – and he, too, hardly got off the ground. Another track opened in America – at Irwindale – and by the end of 1970 there were three prosperous concerns promoting speedway at Costa Mesa, Irwindale and Bakersfield.

But every other venture – or blueprinted venture – fell through and while American speedway had progressed it still has a long way to go.

I am not, though, writing off America as a top class speedway nation. Certainly they are not that now – but within a couple of years and providing their top dozen riders can come to England and adapt to British-style racing, the Yanks could once again become a dominant speedway nation. I feel that is more likely to be in the late seventies than the early seventies though. . . .

16

Where Do We Go From Here?

There's a lot that is wrong with British speedway. But there's also a lot wrong with life!

While I can't do too much to solve the world's problems I do think I can put forward a few ideas that would improve speedway in Britain.

Basically I consider that a lack of respect is one of the major reasons for much that is wrong with the sport. A lack of respect between riders and promoters. A lack of respect between promoters and riders. And a lack of respect between the people who really do count in the long run – supporters – and promoters.

There is very little that I can do to solve the third aspect of lack of respect but certainly there is much I can suggest to solve points one and two.

Travelling around the country I believe I am in a position to comment on the oh-so-apparent lack of respect between promoters and riders.

With very few exceptions promoters seem to consider that the riders are socially inferior to themselves and this becomes obvious in the way they try to carry out their business.

The classic example is the condition of many of the tracks in Britain. Some of them are kept in good condition. Well maintained. Smooth. Safe. And conducive to good racing.

Others are more suited to scrambles or trials riding. It seems to me that some promoters honestly believe that the rougher their track the better the supporter will like it.

I believe this is a fallacy. As far as I am concerned I will race on any track no matter how rough, but I know scores of riders who give far below their best if a track is bumpy and rough.

In the dressing rooms before a meeting they will openly admit that they aren't going to try. I don't blame them. The only reason I ride rough tracks is because I know I have the ability to look after myself on them.

But who can blame a man if he decides it is easier to pull out of a tight position rather than risk the possibility of serious injury which would not only cause physical pain but great financial hardship?

After all what use is a man lying in a hospital bed with a broken leg in plaster? He's certainly a burden on the state . . . on his family . . . and on himself.

But can you drum this into the average Mr Promoter? It seems not, for rather than improve, the standard of tracks has dropped during the past five years or so.

There is always an exception and I must say that whenever I have ridden at a number of tracks – particularly Belle Vue and Sheffield – I have never found the racing surface anything but 100 per cent ideal.

I believe it is no coincidence that both tracks have big crowds every week of the season and racing at these two centres is always exciting and close.

As far as I am concerned a good track makes for good racing. Conversely a bad track makes for bad racing. While it would be stretching a point and sensationalising something that does not need sensationalising to say that riders have been killed because of bad tracks I am firmly convinced that a number of my colleagues have been seriously injured because a promoter was not concerned enough to make his track as good as it should have been.

Until a promoter is made to pay an injured rider while he is in hospital or laid up at home I don't think we will ever get to the situation where every track is ideal. It is a pity but it is a fact of speedway life which I must accept.

The Speedway Control Board, too, could pay far greater attention to the question of a track's condition. To some extent they have paid lip service to this ideal by appointing a track inspector. But the man with the job, former English international Bill Kitchen is, in my opinion, seriously limited in his powers.

I would like to see him given the authority to close a track down on the spot. He should be able to inspect a track and if it isn't as good as it should be, order that no racing take place on that track until the proper maintenance is carried out.

Then, and only then, would a promoter be forced to bring his racing surface up to scratch. Because then, and only then, not to do so would lose him money.

As it is a promoter with a bad track spends less than a promoter with a good track because it stands to reason that less work is needed to keep a bad track in a bad condition than to keep a good track in a good condition.

I realise that this may read like a sweeping condemnation of the condition of Britain's speedway tracks. And that is exactly what it is meant to be.

Moving away from the track the conditions which riders have to accept leave a lot to be desired. In Germany and on the continent I willingly agree to compete in meetings with frugal changing facilities. This is purely because it is a once-a-year happening.

Not in Britain where dressing room facilities at most tracks are far below the standard set by even the most junior of professional soccer clubs.

Few, if any, stadiums catering solely for speedway as the sole human sport have a communal bath where the riders can lounge about soaking away the aches and pains of an evening's hard work.

Most have a few showers but it is always a case of share – or wait your turn. By comparison when I visit those tracks built around a soccer pitch, I'm constantly amazed at the apparent comfort afforded to a football player.

All too often money spent on changing facilities is the last – and I should imagine the smallest – expenditure on a promoter's budget. Again I feel the Control Board should step in and refuse to licence any track that does not conform with a set of laid-down rules and regulations governing this type of facility.

At one track in 1969, for instance, riders had to wash in ONE wash-basin! Imagine it – twenty or so riders crowding around a solitary wash-bowl.

Continuing along the same line, there is a rule in the regulations governing speedway that every track should have covered accommodation in the pit area. A number of tracks would fail this acid test and yet are licensed, when it states quite clearly that no track shall be allowed to operate unless it fulfils all requirements.

Again the Control Board appears to turn a blind eye in this respect.

Perhaps it is a pity that the British promoters haven't taken a leaf out of the book of their Russian counterparts who provided covered, and centrally heated, pits accommodation for every rider in the World Ice Speedway Championship!

Perhaps the points I have so far raised may seem relatively unimportant and petty points on which to dwell. Individually it may be so. But collectively – and taking into account other similar factors – it only goes to show the disdain with which some promoters threat the riders.

Had I been working under such intolerable conditions in a factory or shop I would probably have been out on strike a long, long time ago! And undoubtedly my employer would have had a visit from a Government or local council officials with strict orders on what should be done!

It is this type of thing which shows a promoter's basic lack of respect for a rider. I am probably better treated than most because of my world rating . . . but I know some riders who are pulled and pushed at every turn by their promoter.

Is it any wonder then that the rider has no real respect for his boss?

This also stems from the image that a promoter portrays. Someone like Mr Ronnie Greene or Mr Charles Ochiltree commands the respect of everyone. I admire them both as businessmen, gentlemen and speedway promoters.

For others I do not have the same high regard. I remember well one promoter turning to Mr Greene and asking pointedly: 'Why do they always call you Mister? They never call me that.'

In a nutshell I think that sums up the rider-promoter relationship. Some you can call Mister – others you can't.

Outside this special relationship there are many other things which could be done to improve speedway. Far more time and money should be spent on fostering the sport's image outside the defined circle of people who watch speedway.

When was there any concentrated television advertising campaign to attract new fans to the sport? I can't remember one.

Too many promoters seem more concerned about ensuring that a business rival doesn't make a bigger profit than himself than in endeavouring to provide an increase of business all round.

I am sure a TV advertising drive would benefit all speedway tracks but I despair of ever seeing it operated. Dealings with the national press, too, are on a low-key level.

It would seem that few promoters go out of their way to encourage and feed national newspaper reporters. Instead they are more likely to complain that another track appears to get more publicity than they do.

Most national newspapers have been increasing their coverage of the sport in recent seasons and it is a welcome trend. Often I wonder how much quicker this trend would have been followed if there have been a little more give-and-take on the side of the promoters. But really that is another problem that can only be tackled at some depth with foresight and by employing a professional journalist or public relations man much in the same way as many of the country's leading soccer clubs.

Perhaps the greatest change I would like to see in speedway concerns the national approach to the sport. Parochially many promoters are happy to see one of their own track riders selected for an international – but that is where their interest ends.

All too often sides are picked on a haphazard formula that seems to have no beginning and no end. Compare the preparation that the Iron Curtain riders have before a World Final or big international match, with the British approach.

The Poles or Russians spend weeks in practice learning each others strengths and weaknesses. Riders are paired off to try and learn as much about the other as possible for future internationals.

In Britain a team is picked. And they don't meet until ten minutes before the meeting is due to start.

If Britain is to remain at the top of the speedway tree there must be far more thought paid to training of riders. Not only at the ground floor but at an international level.

I would like to see a party of ten or a dozen selected and allowed to train together rather like Sir Alf Ramsey's now famous soccer training sessions.

A man – an ex-rider preferably who understands the problems of riding – should be appointed in charge of the squad and it should be his responsibility to produce the goods (international victories) otherwise he would be replaced.

The World Team Cup – rightly regarded as a major international event in every country except Britain it seems – should be the national goal every year.

A squad of riders should be selected to attack that goal – and they should succeed. Wherever the final is being held those riders should spend a week or so practising on that track.

Or if that track isn't available another track that is almost identical in shape, size and texture. If the meeting is in Poland the party should be flown out to Poland and after practice the final team should be chosen.

Instead five riders are picked for the meeting . . . and not always the best five riders. No attempt is ever made to ask a rider's advice on selection.

Without being too big-headed I consider I am in a better position to assess a rider's chances of doing well in a country like Poland than a promoter. Simply because I've ridden in that country whereas some of the promoters who select the team haven't even been to the country.

Of course it would be wrong and foolish to suggest a rider picks an international team. I am not asking for that. But I do think it might help if advice was sought.

Everything should be geared to a climax. For an individual rider it should be the World Final. For the country it should be the World Team Cup. For a club side the League championship.

Instead a year's fixture list is clouded with fancy-titled meaningless meetings. The Pride of the Midlands. The Champion of Champions. Meaningless meetings that are built up to World Championship proportions by individual promoters.

Surely it would be a better idea to have a series of qualifying rounds for a meaningful overall title. Then each track would be part of a whole and a working part of a whole rather than an often insignificant abstraction out on a limb.

It is only by working together and pulling in the same direction that speedway is going to continue to advance.

In the past ten years great strides have been made in this direction and I sincerely hope that they will continue to advance even more so than in the past.

While this chapter has been mainly critical of the current set up I hope it has been intelligent and well-reasoned criticism. There is still much that is wrong in speedway. But there is far more that is right.

And it is only by channelling what is right in the same direction and endeavouring to eradicate what is wrong, that the sport will prosper still further.

Criticisms I may have but at the end of the day I still consider speedway the best sport in the world. Without it I would be lost. But I try not to let that disguise the true facts.

There is still much to be done in speedway; a lot of progress yet to be made.

But as the philosophers have said where there's a will there's a way. And as far as I'm concerned there is a way. . . .

Appendix

IVAN MAUGER – FACTS AND FIGURES

THE WORLD CHAMPIONSHIP STORY:

1957

Did not compete.

1958

17th July	Qualifying round	Ipswich	3 pts
19th July	Qualifying round	Coventry	9 pts

1959–1962

Did not compete. Not riding in Britain.

1963

10th June	Provincial round	Newcastle	14 pts	Won
14th June	Provincial round	Wolverhampton	15 pts	Won
22nd June	Provincial Final	Edinburgh	14 pts	Won
2nd July	Qualifying round	Swindon	6 pts	
4th July	Qualifying round	Southampton	5 pts	
5th July	Qualifying round	Oxford	2 pts	

1964

Did not compete – at the time the Provincial League was unlicensed and riders not eligible for the World Championship.

1965

14th June	Qualifying round	Newcastle	11 pts
18th June	Qualifying round	Glasgow	12 pts
19th June	Qualifying round	Edinburgh	11 pts
30th July	British semi-final	Glasgow	11 pts
31st Aug.	British Final	West Ham	5 pts

1966

23rd May	Qualifying round	Newcastle	15 pts	Won
24th May	Qualifying round	Long Eaton	12 pts	
27th May	Qualifying round	Hackney Wick	11 pts	
15th June	British semi-final	Halifax	9 pts	
27th June	British Final	Wimbledon	11 pts	
14th July	Nordic/British Final	Sheffield	13 pts	
3rd Sept.	European Final	Wembley	14 pts	Won
23rd Sept.	World Final	Gothenburg, Sweden	11 pts	Fourth

1967

12th May	Qualifying round	Hackney Wick	15 pts	Won
13th May	Qualifying round	Cradley Heath	10 pts	
22nd May	Qualifying round	Newcastle	15 pts	Won
13th July	British semi-final	Wimbledon	10 pts	
22nd Aug.	British Final	West Ham	13 pts	
16th Sept.	World Final	Wembley, England	13 pts	Third

1968

25th May	Qualifying round	Belle Vue	15 pts	Won
27th May	Qualifying round	Newcastle	15 pts	Won
28th May	Qualifying round	West Ham	13 pts	
2nd July	British semi-final	Poole	14 pts	Won
11th July	British Final	Wimbledon	15 pts	Won
6th Aug.	Nordic/British Final	West Ham	15 pts	Won
25th Aug.	European Final	Wroclaw, Poland	10 pts	
6th Sept.	World Final	Gothenburg, Sweden	15 pts	Won

1969

21st May	Qualifying round	Poole	14 pts	
22nd May	Qualifying round	Wimbledon	12 pts	
24th May	Qualifying round	Belle Vue	15 pts	Won
26th June	British semi-final	Sheffield	14 pts	Won
5th Aug.	British Final	West Ham	11 pts	
13th Sept.	World Final	Wembley, London	14 pts	Won

1970

25th Apr.	Qualifying round	Belle Vue	11 pts	
27th Apr.	Qualifying round	Exeter	15 pts	Won
28th Apr.	Qualifying round	West Ham	15 pts	Won
19th May	British semi-final	Leicester	15 pts	Won
9th June	British Final	West Ham	14 pts	Won
1st July	Nordic/British Final	Coventry	10 pts	
19th July	European Final	Leningrad, U.S.S.R.	14 pts	Won
6th Sept.	World Final	Wroclaw, Poland	15 pts	Won

WORLD CHAMPIONSHIP HONOURS – 1958–1970

World Champion, 1968, 1969, 1970.

European Champion, 1966, 1970.

Nordic/British Champion, 1968.

British Champion, 1968, 1970.

Race by race details World Finals, 1968, 1969, 1970.

1968

Ivan Mauger (Newcastle and New Zealand)	3–3–3–3–3–	15
Barry Briggs (Swindon and New Zealand)	2–2–3–3–2–	12
Edward Jancarz (Poland)	1–3–1–3–3–	11
Gennady Kurilenko (U.S.S.R.)	2–3–3–1–2–	11
Torbjorn Harryson (Newport and Sweden)	3–3–2–1–1–	10
Pawel Waloszek (Poland)	F–2–3–2–3–	10
Anders Michanek (Leicester and Sweden)	3–1–2–2–1–	9
Hasse Holmkvist (Wolverhampton and Sweden)	1–2–2–2–2–	9
Ove Fundin (Sweden)	3–0–1–0–3–	7
Gunnar Malmkvist (Sweden)	0–2–1–3–1–	7
Antoni Woryna (Poland)	2–1–0–1–1–	5
Martin Ashby (Exeter and England)	2–1–0–2–0–	5
Reidar Eide (Coatbridge and Norway)	0–0–2–1–F–	3
Jerzy Trzeszkowski (Poland)	F–1–0–0–2–	3
Bernt Persson (Coatbridge and Sweden)	e–0–1–0–0–	1
Nigel Boocock (Coventry and England)	1–0–0–F–e–	1

1969

Ivan Mauger (Belle Vue and New Zealand)	3–3–3–3–2–	14
Barry Briggs (Swindon and New Zealand)	3–2–2–1–3–	11
Soren Sjosten (Belle Vue and Sweden)	3–F–2–3–3–	11
Nigel Boocock (Coventry and England)	3–2–3–1–1–	10
Hasse Holmkvist (Sweden)	2–1–3–2–2–	10
Edward Jancarz (Poland)	1–1–1–3–3–	9
Ove Fundin (Sweden)	2–2–2–3–0–	9
Ken McKinlay (West Ham and Scotland)	1–3–3–0–0–	7
Andrzej Pogorzelski (Poland)	0–3–1–2–1–	7
Jan Mucha (Poland)	1–0–2–2–2–	7
Ronnie Moore (Wimbledon and New Zealand)	2–1–1–1–1–	6
Henryk Glucklick (Poland)	0–0–0–2–3–	5
Valerij Klementiev (U.S.S.R.)	0–3–F–e–1–	4
Torbjorn Harryson (Sweden)	2–2–F——	4
Zbighiew Podlecki (Poland) RESERVE	1–2———	3
Andrzej Wyglenda (Poland)	0–1–1–0–0–	2
Howard Cole (Kings Lynn and England)	1–0–0–0–0–	1

1970

Ivan Mauger (Belle Vue and New Zealand)	3–3–3–3–3–	15
Pawel Waloszek (Poland)	3–3–3–2–3–	14
Antoni Woryna (Poland)	3–3–2–3–2–	13
Soren Sjosten (Belle Vue and Sweden)	2–3–1–3–F–	9
Henryk Glucklick (Poland)	2–2–3–2–0–	9
Valerij Klementiev (U.S.S.R.)	0–1–1–3–3–	8
Barry Briggs (Swindon and New Zealand)	2–1–0–1–3–	7
Andrzej Wyglenda (Poland)	1–0–3–2–1–	7
Anders Michanek (Newcastle and Sweden)	0–1–2–2–2–	7
Ole Olsen (Wolverhampton and Denmark)	3–2–0–e–1–	6
Jan Mucha (Poland)	1–2–0–1–2–	6
Hans Jurgen Fritz (East Germany)	1–0–1–1–2–	5
Valeriz Gordeev (U.S.S.R.)	2–1–1–0–1–	5
Edmung Migos (Poland) RESERVE	2–1–1–F–0–	4
Gennady Kurilenko (U.S.S.R.)	F–2–F——	2
Zygmund Friedek (Poland)	F–0–2–F—	2
Trevor Hedge (Wimbledon and England)	e–0–F–e—	0

(Abbreviations: F=fell; e=engine failure)

World Best Pairs Champion, 1969, 1970.
World Team Cup, member winning side, 1968

BRITISH LEAGUE SCORING RECORD, 1965-1970*

		M	*R*	*1st*	*2nd*	*3rd*	*4th*	*Pts*	*B.P.*	*Total*	*Ave.*
1965	Newcastle **	20	78	34	24	10	10	160	12	172	8.85
1966	Newcastle	41	180	99	48	14	19	407	15	422	9.36
1967	Newcastle	36	166	99	30	20	17	377	10	387	9.32
1968	Newcastle	36	158	139	14	2	3	447	2	449	11.37
1969	Belle Vue	37	158	145	10	1	2	456	5	461	11.67
1970	Belle Vue	40	170	142	21	3	4	471	4	481	11.40

*includes Knock-out Cup matches
**includes one match as guest for Edinburgh – four rides, 9 points

CROSS-SECTION OF OTHER CHIEF HONOURS (1965–1970)

Internationale Winner, 1970
Northern Riders Champion, 1967, 1968, 1969
Silver Sash Match Race Champion, 1968, 1969
Golden Helmet Match Race Champion, 1970
Scotianapolis Winner, 1969, 1970
Scottish Open Champion, 1970
Winner Leningrad Cup (U.S.S.R.) 1969
Winner Golden Key of Bremen (Germany), 1968, 1969, 1970
Winner World Champion of World Champions (New Zealand), 1970
Winner Lokeren Memorial Trophy, 1970

Honours before formation of British League in 1965 include Provincial League Riders Champion, 1963, 1964. Silver Sash Match Race Holder 1963, 1964. Northern Riders Champion, 1964. Australian Long Track Champion, 1962. Victorian Champion, 1962, 1963.

Index